THE GLORIOUS CHASE

❖

A Celebration of Foxhunting

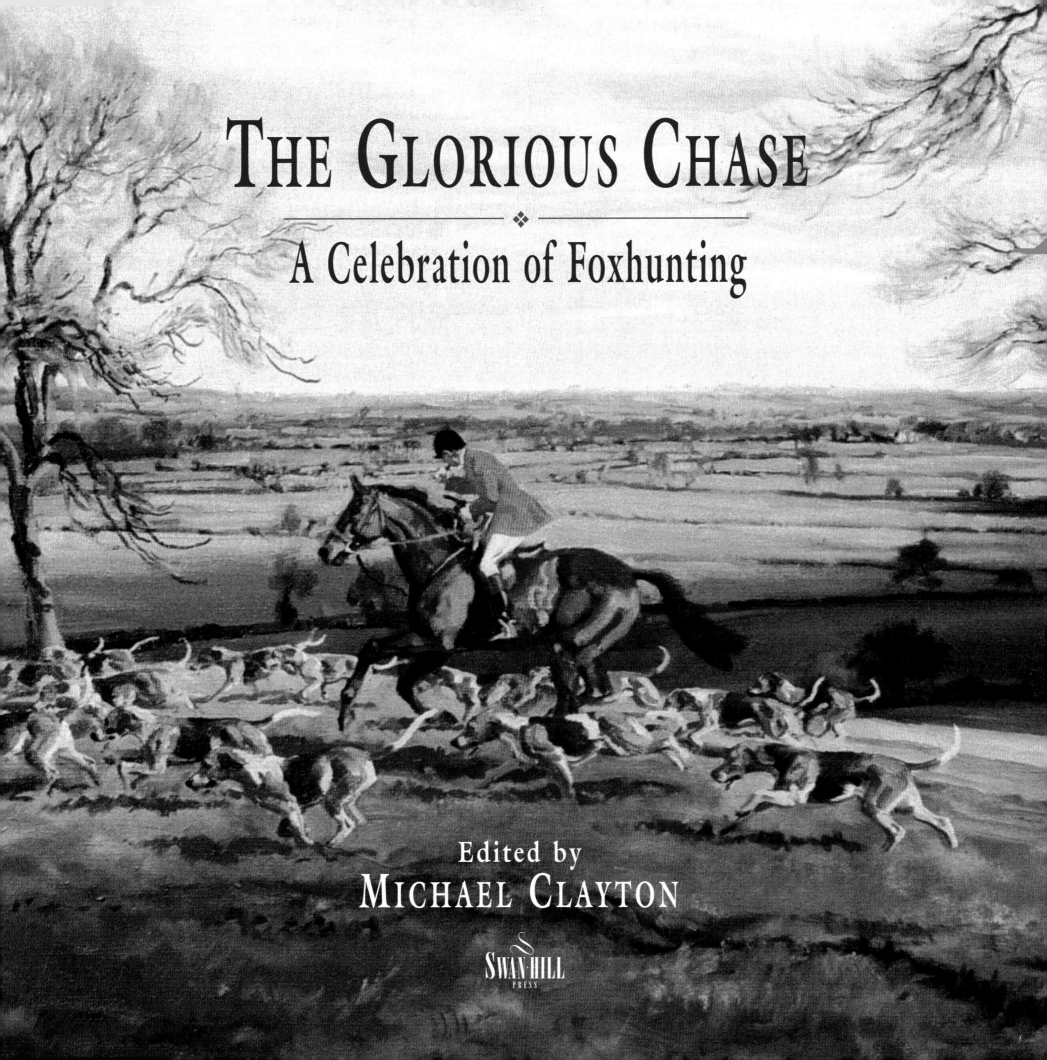

THE GLORIOUS CHASE

A Celebration of Foxhunting

Edited by

MICHAEL CLAYTON

SWAN HILL
PRESS

First published in the UK in 2005
by Swan Hill Press, an imprint of Quiller Publishing Ltd

British Library Cataloguing-in-Publication Data

A catalogue record for this book
is available from the British Library

ISBN 1 904057 75 6

Printed in China

Swan Hill Press
An imprint of Quiller Publishing Ltd
Wykey House, Wykey, Shrewsbury, SY4 1JA
Tel: 01939 261616 Fax: 01939 261606
E-mail: info@quillerbooks.com
Website: www.swanhillbooks.com

Contents

— ❖ —

SWEET CRY OF HOUNDS...

HUNTSMEN ALL

THE FUN OF IT ...

LIST OF ILLUSTRATIONS

Acknowledgements

— ❖ —

I am much indebted in compiling this book to The Earl Bathurst who has kindly given permission for excerpts previously published in *The Foxhunter's Bedside Book,* the delightful anthology so carefully and knowledgeably compiled by his mother, the late Lady Apsley MFH,OBE. She was a Joint Master of the VWH (1946-56), and MP for Bristol Central (1942-45) in the national war-time government. All this was accomplished while she was crippled in a wheelchair from a hunting accident in 1932. She was an outstanding side-saddle horsewoman until her accident. Lady Apsley became an MP after her husband, Lord Apsley DSO, MC was killed on active service in 1942.

The Foxhunter's Bedside Book was published in 1949 by Eyre and Spottiswoode and has long had a cherished place on my bookshelves. George Pearson, proprietor and publisher of *Baily's Hunting Directory*, generously gave permission for excerpts from his publications *Great Days (1997)* and *Baily's Hunting Companion(1994).* Other permissions include Hugh Robards (*Foxhunting – A Life in Hunt Service,* Derrydale Press, 2000); Norman Fine, publisher of Derrydale Press (*Rycroft on Hounds, Hunting and Cou),* Derrydale Press,2001*;* Christopher Sporburg, (Sir Stephen Hastings, *Drums of Memory,* 1994, Leo Cooper*).* Other modern sources include two books under my own copyright, *Foxford's Hunting Companion,* Country Life Books 1978*;* and *Foxhunting in Paradise,* John Murray 1993. Simon Blow (*Fields Elysian*, J M Dent 1983); J A Allen (publishers of *Magic of the Quorn* by Ulrica Murray Smith). Every effort has been made to seek permissions from copyright owners but in some cases this has not been possible. The Publisher will gladly include any omissions in future editions. I am most grateful to my friends John King, for permission to include his superb paintings of the Portman, Burton and Blackmore and Spankford Vale, and Jim Meads for his marvellous photographs, likewise to John Minoprio, Amanda Lockhart and Leslie Lane. Frederick J. Haycock's excellent Quorn picture was presented to me by Horse and Hound contributors in our centenary year, 1984.

The Publisher wishes to thank Mr Bryn Parry for his original suggestion which led to the publication of this book.

INTRODUCTION

❖

Far too many Britons have learned about foxhunting in recent years only in sound-bite arguments on radio and TV as the long, wearying hunting saga ground its way towards the ban achieved on 18 February, 2005, by a Labour dominated, anti-libertarian majority of the House of Commons. Prejudiced and ignorant of country life, and full of spite from some outworn class war, these MPs were willing to ram the ban past the honourable and well considered objections of the Lords, by dubious use of the draconian Parliament Act.

The Hunting Act has rightly been condemned as appallingly drafted in seeking a ban which could not possibly benefit the fox; it fails utterly as meaningful animal welfare law, and if it remains forever on the statute book would lead to the near extermination of the fox in our countryside as it falls prey to unmonitored control by the gun, the snare and poison, without the observation of a close season in the summer. The role of Hunts in maintaining the multitude of hunting coverts which created the very shape of our landscape throughout three hundred years, was totally ignored by the Blair government and its parliamentary party.

Foxhunting has evoked its own literature and art for some three hundred years. They tell an infinitely more attractive and accurate, rounded account of the sport than the shrill of cacophony of abuse hurled by hard-core animal rights extremists.

In the pages of perceptive writers, foxhunting emerges as a pastime which has added inestimably to Britons' appreciation of their own countryside, and as a genuine contributor to the conservation of foxes. Its place in our rural culture is long established in our language and our customs, many of which have survived until today.

There is a beauty and a passion in foxhunting, but there is charm and humour too. No two days are alike; no two hunting countries are identical. The sport produced some of the finest depictions on canvas of the English landscape, and some of the most enduring descriptions of sporting endeavour.

In these selections I have striven to give a taste of such pleasures in the hope they will add lustre to the memories of many who hunt, and that they will stimulate modern Britons to explore further the heritage of books and pictures evoked by foxhunting – an innocent enjoyment of our countryside which embittered politicians have sought to besmirch and destroy.

Robert Smith Surtees, arguably only second to Dickens as a nineteenth century novelist, created in John Jorrocks one of our greatest literary characters: the huge, bouncing Cockney grocer who learned to thrill to the Chase on the Surrey Hills, south of London.

Jorrocks illustrates the classless appeal of foxhunting, and in *Handley Cross* the sheer common-sense of his famous 'sporting lectors' survives the test of time: '...it ar'nt that I loves the fox less, but that I loves the 'ound more... .The 'oss loves the 'ound, and I loves both; and it is that love wot brings me to these parts, to follow the all-glorious callin' of the chase.'

Nimrod's exciting, breathless accounts of epic runs across Leicestershire contrast with the luminous evocations of Edwardian country life in Kent and Sussex achieved by Siegfried Sassoon in his wonderful *Memoirs of a Foxhunting Man*.

There are some prosaic, work-a-day descriptions of foxhunting in this anthology because it is essential that the skills of the huntsman as a naturalist as well as a controller and trainer of hounds, are recognised and preserved. The words of 'Master' the 10th Duke of Beaufort, Sir Peter Farquhar, and Ronnie Wallace convey something of the science as well as the art of foxhunting.

I have included several contemporary contributions because foxhunting was criminalised in 2005 while it was still a thriving and popular sport, still achieving new generations of recruits to the hunting field. Thousands of children were riding to hounds on the last 'legal' day's hunting, and it is their birthright which is imperilled.

I am profoundly grateful to Andrew Johnston, head of Quiller Publishing, for so generously proposing the publication of this book from which he is donating profit to the Countryside Alliance's Campaign for Hunting. As one who has been fortunate to enjoy a life-time of foxhunting in so many hunting countries I hope *The Glorious Chase* makes its own contribution to the restoration of our sport as an activity approved by the law in a more enlightened and tolerant society.

I have included the famous 'Fox's Prophecy' in this anthology as being more appropriate than ever to the present plight of our country – and hope that readers will gain comfort from the fox's firm prediction that:

> 'Again the smiling hedgerow
> Shall field from field divide;
> Again among the woodlands
> The scarlet troop shall ride.'

MICHAEL CLAYTON
Rutland, July 2005

FOXHUNTING - THE SPORT

A Sporting Lector

❖

Precisely at eight o'clock Mr Jorrocks ascended the platform, attended by Captain Doleful, Roger Swizzle, Romeo Simpkins, and Abel Snorem, and was received with the most enthusiastic cheering. He wore the full-dress uniform of the hunt; sky-blue coat lined with pink silk, canary-coloured shorts, and white silk stockings.

His neckcloth and waistcoat were white, and a finely plaited shirt-frill protruded through the stand-up collar of the latter.

Bunches of white ribbon dangled at his knees. In his hand he held a roll of notes, while some books of reference and a tumbler of brandy and water, were placed by Benjamin on a table at the back of the platform. Benjamin had on his new red frock with blue collar, cord breeches, and white stockings.

After bowing most familiarly to the company, Mr Jorrocks cleared his voice with a substantial hem, and then addressed the meeting.

'Beloved 'earers ! beloved I may call you, for though I have not the pleasure of knowin' many of you, I hope werry soon to make your intimate acquaintance. Beloved 'earers, I say, I have come 'ere this evenin' for the double purpose of seeing you, and instructin' of you on those matters that have brought me to this your beautiful and salubrisome town. (Cheers.)

'Beautiful I may call it, for its architectural proportions are grand, and salubrisome it must be when it boasts so many cheerful, vigorous countenances as I now see gathered around me. (Loud applause.) And if by my comin', I shall spread the great light of sportin' knowledge, and enable you to preserve those glowin' mugs when far removed from these waters, then shall I be a better doctor than either Swizzle or Sebastian, and the day that drew John Jorrocks from the sugars of retirement in Great Coram Street will henceforth remain red-lettered in the mental calendar of his existence. (Loud cheers.) Red-lettered did I say ? Ah! wot a joyous colour to denote a great and glorious ewent ! Believe me there is no colour like red – no sport like 'unting.

'Blue coats and canaries,' observed Mr Jorrocks looking down at his legs, 'are well enough for dancin' in, but the man wot does much dancin' will not do much 'unting. But to business – Lectorin' is all the go – and why should sportin' be excluded ? Is it because sportin' is its own champion ? Away with the idea ! Are there no pints on which grey experience can show the beacon lights to 'ot youth and indiscretion? Assuredly there are! Full then of hardour – full of keenness, one pure concentrated essence of 'unting, John Jorrocks comes to enlighten all men capable of instruction on pints that all wish to be considered conversant with.

'Well did that great man, I think it was Walter Scott, but if it warn't, 'twas little Bartley, the bootmaker, say, that there was no young man wot would not rather have a himputation on his

'The Quorn Hunt, Plate V: Snob is Beat', print by F.C. Lewis after Henry Alken, 1835. Poor Snob is reduced to opening a gate in this famous picture, while some of the best known riders of the day – including Mr Holyoake, Captain Ross and Mr White – fly the obstacle.

'His Lordship has it all to himself' – John Leech's engraving of Lord Scamperdale, Master of the Flat Hat Hunt, enjoying a great hunt, in Mr Sponge's Sporting Tour by R. S. Surtees.

morality than on his 'ossmanship, and yet, how few there are wot really know anything about the matter! Oh, but if hignorance be bliss 'ow 'appy must they be! (Loud cheers and laughter.)

''Unting is the sport of kings, the image of war without its guilt, and only five-and-twenty per cent of its danger! In that word, ''unting,' what a ramification of knowledge is compressed!

'The choice of an 'oss – the treatment of him when got – the groomin' at home, the ridin' abroad – the boots, the breeches, the saddle, the bridle, the 'ound, the 'untsman, the feeder, the Fox!

'Oh, how that beautiful word, Fox, gladdens my 'eart and warms the declinin' embers of my age. (Cheers.) The 'oss and the 'ound were made for each other, and natur' threw in the Fox as a connectin' link between the two. (Loud cheers.) He's perfect symmetry, and my affection for him, is a perfect paradox.

'In the summer I loves him with all hardour of affection; not an 'air of his beautiful 'ead would I hurt; the sight of him is more glorious nor the Lord Mayor's show! but when the hautumn comes – when the brownin' copse and cracklin' stubble proclaim the farmer's fears are past, then, dash my vig, 'ow I glories in pursuing him to destruction, and holdin' him above the bayin' pack ! (Loud cheers.)

'And yet,' added Mr Jorrocks thoughtfully, 'it ar'nt that I loves the fox less, but that I loves the 'ound more, as the chap says in the play, when he sticks his friend in the gizzard. (Roars of laughter and applause.)

'The 'oss loves the 'ound, and I loves both; and it is that love wot brings me to these parts, to follow the all-glorious callin' of the chase, and to enlighten all men capable of illumination. To-night I shall instruct you with a lecture on dealin'.

' "O, who shall counsel a man in the choice of a wife or an 'oss?" asked that inspired writer, the renowned Johnny Lawrence, "The buyer has need of a hundred eyes, the seller of but one," says another equestrian conjuror.

'Who can take up an 'oss book and read 'bout splints, and spavins, and stringalts, and corns, and cuttin', and farcy, and dropsy, and fever, and thrushes, and grease, and gripes, and mallenders, and sallenders, and ring-bones, and roarin', etcetera, etceterorem, without a shudder lest such a complication of evils should fall to his lot? Who can expect a perfect 'oss, when he sees what an infinity of hills they are heirs to? I hopes I haven't come to 'Andley Cross to inform none on you what an 'oss is, nor to explain that its component parts are four legs, a backbone, an 'ead, a neck, a tail, and other etceteras, too numerous to insert in an 'and-bill, as old Georgy Robins used to say.

''Eavens, wot a lot of rubbish has been written about 'osses!' continued the worthy lecturer, casting up his eyes. 'Away with all such rubbish, say I! John Jorrocks is the only real enlightened sapient sportsman ; and 'ere, 'ere from this lofty heminence I hurls defiance at the whole tribe of word-manglin', grammar-stranglin', cotation crammin' cocks! bids them to a grand tilt or tournament of jaw, where hevery man may do his best, and I'll make mincemeat of them all-catermauchously chaw them up, as the Americans say.' (Loud cheers.)

R.S. Surtees, *Handley Cross*

Foxhunting and the Sporting Artist

❖

Nothing reflects the new status of fox hunting better than the attention paid to it by painters and writers. The eighteenth century saw both the beginnings of sporting journalism and a flowering of sporting art.

As early as 1723 Wootton was painting foxhounds for their aristocratic owners. In 1792 one of the greatest English artists, George Stubbs, painted one of the greatest English hounds – Lord Yarborough's 'Ringwood', pride of the Brocklesby kennels.

Just as the hunter owed a great deal to the racehorse, so the sporting artist who painted hunting scenes owed a great deal to the patronage of the racing aristocracy. Ben Marshall (1767–1835), who painted that great northern MFH, Lord Darlington, visited Newmarket. 'I have a good reason for going. I discover many a man who will pay me fifty guineas for painting his horse who thinks ten guineas too much to pay for painting his wife.' Rich racehorse owners had commissioned John Wootton (1678–1764) to paint their horses; his portraits, based on traditional poses observed from treatises on equitation and Ruini's *Anatomy* (published in 1598), were wooden.

It was George Stubbs, obsessed as he was with equine anatomy – the stench of his putrefying models got him into trouble with his neighbours – who first made a horse look like an individual animal.

Stubbs' early patrons were largely rich racehorse owners born around 1730 and who had grown up with the Jockey Club as the centre of their lives. To a man who, like Grosvenor, spent £7,000 a year on racing, a hundred for a picture of a favourite horse was nothing. But Stubbs was too profound an artist to become a mere sporting illustrator in the sense that Ben Marshall was, or that his pupil, John Ferneley, was to become.

Like Stubbs, George Morland, who died of drink in 1804 at the age of forty-two, knew the hunting and racing world. Indeed Morland suffered from both hunters and race-goers at Margate in 1785. Riding as an amateur he won a race only to be beaten up by the crowd who had bet on his opponent. Then he lost all his sitters to the hunting field. 'Last Monday week almost everyone in Margate was drunk by reason of the Freemasons meeting and fox hunt.'

A strong impression remains, after looking at eighteenth-century pictures, that fox hunting was still a staid business and that fields were small. James Seymour's (d.1752) *The Chase* looks something like a modern fox hunt, and one of Tilleman's (d. 1734) hunting pictures has a man coming off over a gate. Both were painted early in the century. Yet the general impression remains: there are no large fields rushing at fences, no signs of a really 'fast thing'. We have to wait for Henry Alken, who worked from 1820 to 1850, to introduce us to the world of the

'The Toast', print by Cooper and Sutherland after Henry Alken: last of a set of seven foxhunting scenes. Hunt members toast a gallant fox hunted that day. The fox's brush is held aloft by the man proposing the toast.

riding disaster, of large numbers of 'red-coated gentlemen in every species of discomfort'. According to 'The Druid' (H.H. Dixon), Mr Meynell's horses used to rear on their hind legs, and jump stiles standing, 'in the most sober and comfortable way . . . getting through the country, not over it'.

Does Mr Meynell's world, as reflected in sporting art, appear so quiet and so classically ordered because artists had not learnt the convention that was to be used to give the illusion of horses at speed – the 'rocking horse' with fore and hind legs stretched out, impossibly out of contact with the ground as photography was to show?

Or was it because the dashing rider was a creation of the Romantic movement, or a facet of the exhibitionism of Regency bucks, the Corinthians whose Leicestershire antics made Melton Mowbray the hunting capital of England but an unsuitable place for a respectable lady?

Raymond Carr, *English Foxhunting 1976*

'Returning Home by Moonlight', print by R. Havell and Son after James Pollard, 1817: last of a set of four, the first entitled 'A Celebrated Fox Hunt'.

First Day

❖

By all the laws of aunthood we should by now have been well on our way home. But Dixon was making a real day of it. The afternoon hunt was going to be a serious affair. There never appeared to be any doubt about that. The field was reduced to about forty riders, and the chattersome contingent seemed to have gone home. We all went into the covert and remained close together at one end. Dixon got off and tightened my girths, which had got very loose (as I ought to have noticed). A resolute-looking lady in a tall hat drew her veil down after taking a good pull at the flask which she handed back to her groom. Hard-faced men rammed their hats on to their heads and sat silently in the saddle as though, for the first time in the day, they really meant business. My heart was in my mouth and it had good reason to be there. Lord Dumborough was keeping an intent eye on the ride which ran through the middle of the covert. 'Cut along up to the top end, Charlie,' he remarked without turning his head; and a gaunt, ginger-haired man in a weather-stained scarlet coat went off up the covert in a squelchy canter.

'That's Mr. Macdoggart,' said Dixon in a low voice, and my solemnity increased as the legendary figure vanished on its mysterious errand.

Meanwhile the huntsman was continuing his intermittent yaups as he moved along the other side of the wood. Suddenly his cheers of encouragement changed to a series of excited shoutings. 'Hoick-holler, hoick-holler, hoick-holler!' he yelled, and then blew his horn loudly; this was followed by an outbreak of vociferation from the hounds, and soon they were in full cry across the covert. I sat there petrified by my private feelings; Sheila showed no symptoms of agitation; she merely cocked her ears well forward and listened.

And then, for the first time, I heard a sound which has thrilled generations of fox-hunters to their marrow. From the far side of the wood came the long shrill screech (for which it is impossible to find an adequate word) which signifies that one of the whips has viewed the fox quitting the covert. 'Gone Away' it meant. But before I had formulated the haziest notion about it Lord Dumborough was galloping up the ride and the rest of them were pelting after him as though nothing could stop them. As I happened to be standing well inside the wood and Sheila took the affair into her own control, I was swept along with them, and we emerged on the other side among the leaders.

I cannot claim that I felt either excitement or resolution as we bundled down a long slope of meadowland and dashed helter-skelter through an open gate at the bottom. I knew nothing at all except that I was out of breath and that the air was rushing to meet me, but as I hung on to the reins I was aware that Mr Macdoggart was immediately in front of me. My attitude was an acquiescent one. I have always been inclined to accept life in the form in which it has imposed itself upon me, and on that particular occasion, no doubt, I just felt that I was 'in for it'. It did not so much as occur to me that in following Mr Macdoggart I was setting myself rather a high standard, and when he disappeared over a hedge I took it for granted that I must do the same.

For a moment Sheila hesitated in her stride. (Dixon told me afterwards that I actually hit her as we approached the fence, but I couldn't remember having done so.) Then she collected herself and jumped the fence with a peculiar arching of her back. There was a considerable drop on the other side. Sheila had made no mistake, but as she landed I left the saddle and flew over her head. I had let go of the reins, but she stood stock-still while I sat on the wet ground.

A few moments later Dixon popped over a gap lower down the fence and came to my assistance, and I saw the boy on the chestnut pony come after him and gallop on in a resolute but unhurrying way. I scrambled to my feet, feeling utterly ashamed.

'Whatever made you go for it like that?' asked Dixon, who was quite disconcerted.

'I saw Mr Macdoggart going over it, and I didn't like to stop,' I stammered. By now the whole hunt had disappeared and there wasn't a sound to be heard.

'Well, I suppose we may as well go on.' He laughed as he gave me a leg up. 'Fancy you following Mr Macdoggart over the biggest place in the fence. Good thing Miss Sherston couldn't see you.'

The idea of my aunt seemed to amuse him, and he slapped his knee and chuckled as he led me onward at a deliberate pace. Secretly mortified by my failure I did my best to simulate cheerfulness. But I couldn't forget the other boy and how ridiculous he must have thought me when he saw me rolling about on the ground. I felt as if I must be covered with mud. About half an hour later we found the hunt again, but I can remember nothing more except that it was beginning to get dark and the huntsman, a middle-aged, mulberry-faced man named Jack Pitt, was blowing his horn as he sat in the middle of his hounds. The other boy was actually talking to him – a privilege I couldn't imagine myself promoted to. At that moment I almost hated him for his cocksuredness.

Then, to my surprise, the Master himself actually came up and asked me how far I was from home. In my embarrassment I could only mutter that I didn't know, and Dixon interposed with 'About twelve miles, m'lord,' in his best manner.

'I hear he's quite a young thruster.' . . . The great man glanced at me for a moment with curiosity before he turned away. Not knowing what he meant I went red in the face and thought he was making fun of me.

Now that I have come to the end of my first day's hunting I am tempted to moralize about it. But I have already described it at greater length than I had intended, so I will only remind myself of the tea I had at an inn on the way home. The inn was kept by a friend of Dixon's – an ex-butler who 'had been with Lord Dumborough for years'. I well remember the snug fire-lit parlour where I ate my two boiled eggs, and how the innkeeper and his wife made a fuss over me. Dixon, of course, transferred me to them in my full status of 'one of the quality', and then disappeared to give the horses their gruel and get his own tea in the kitchen. I set off on the ten dark miles home in a glow of satisfied achievement, and we discussed every detail

'The Cotswold at Bagendon, 1945': watercolour by Michael Lyne (1912-89), celebrated sporting artist who lived in the Cotswolds and derived much inspiration from hunting in Gloucestershire.

of the day except my disaster. Dixon had made enquiries about 'the other young gentleman', and had learnt that his name was Milden and that he was staying at Dumborough Park for Christmas. He described him as a proper little sportsman; but I was reticent on the subject. Nor did I refer to the question of our going out with the hounds again. By the time we were home I was too tired to care what anybody in the world thought about me.

Siegfried Sassoon, *Memoirs of a Foxhunting Man* (1928)

THIS IS OUR HERITAGE

❖

This is our heritage; the love of sport,
A fair ambition and a friendly strife,
The rivalry of farm and camp and court
The clean endeavour of a clean hard life.

This is our heritage that none can take:
The gift we hold the gift we give again,
And this the spirit that no time can break
So long as England and her fields remain.

Will H. Ogilvie

Working sketches by Michael Lyne, an example of his great talent as a draughtsman as well as a painter. He continued drawing to the very end of his life.

LOWESLEY HALL

—— ❖ ——

Brother sportsmen, staunch protectionists! rejecting all that's new,
Oh! the future that's impending is a queerish one for you;

For I look'd into its pages and I read the book of fate,
And saw Fox Hunting abolished by an order of the State;

Saw the heavens filled with guano, and the clouds at man's command
Raining down unsavoury liquids for the benefit of land;

Saw the airy Navies earthward bear the planetary swell,
And the long projected railway made from Hanover to H—l;

Saw the landlords yield their acres, after centuries of wrongs,
To the cotton lords, to whom, it's proved, all property belongs;

Queen, Religion, State abandoned, and all flags of party furled
In the government of Cobden and the dotage of the world.

Then shall exiled common sense espouse some other country's cause,
And the rogues shall thrive in England, bonneting the slumb'ring laws.

Sir W. Bromley Davenport MP (1870)

'Optimists at the Meet', 1931, watercolour by Frank Algernon Stewart (1877-1945), a keen foxhunter who lived at Cheltenham. He was a sporting artist who excelled at book illustration as well as painting and whose work was exhibited regularly in London.

THE FOX'S PROPHECY

❖

All nature seemed rejoicing
That glorious morn to see
All seemed to breathe a fresher life
Beast, insect, bird, and tree.

But sound and sight, and beauty
Fell dull on eye and ear;
The huntsman's heart was heavy,
His brow oppressed with care.

High in his stirrups raised he stood,
And long he gazed around,
And breathlessly and anxiously
He listened for a sound.

But naught he heard save song of bird,
Or jay's discordant cry;
Or, when among the tree tops
The wind went murmuring by.

No voice of hound, no sound of horn,
The woods around were mute,
As though the earth had swallowed up
His comrades, man and brute.

He thought 'I must essay to find
My hounds at any cost;
A huntsman who has lost his hounds
Is but a huntsman lost.'

Then round he turned his horse's head,
And shook his bridle free,
When he was aware of an aged fox
That sat beneath a tree.

He raised his eyes in glad surprise,
That huntsman keen and bold
But there was in that fox's look
That made his blood run cold!

He raised his hand to blow his horn
And shout a 'Tally-ho!'
But, mastered by that fox's eye,
His lips refused to blow.

For he was grim, and gaunt of limb,
With age all silvered o'er;
He might have been an Arctic fox
Escaped from Greenland's shore.

But age his vigour had not tamed
Nor dimmed his glittering eye,
That shone with an unearthly fire –
A fire could never die.

And thus the huntsman he addressed,
In tones distinct and clear,
Who heard as they who in a dream
The fairies' music hear.

'Huntsman,' he said – a sudden thrill
Through all his listener ran
To hear a creature of the wood
Speak like a Christian man.

'Last of my race, to me 'tis given
The future to unfold;
To speak the words which never yet
Spake fox of mortal mould.

'In my strong youth, which numbers now
Full many a season back,
How scornfully I shook my brush
Before the Berkeley pack.

'Then deem not that I speak in fear,
Or prophesy in hate;
Too well I know the doom reserved
For all my tribe by fate.

'Too well I know, by wisdom taught,
The existence of my race;
O'er all wide England's green domain
Is bound up with the chase.

'Better in early youth and strength
The race for life to run,
Than poisoned like the noxious rat,
Or slain by felon gun.

'Better by wily sleight and turn
The eager hound to foil,
Than slaughtered by each baser churl,
Who yet shall till the soil.

'For not upon those hills alone
The doom of sport shall fall;
O'er the broad face of England
Creeps the shadow on the wall.

'In England's ancient pulpits
Lay orators shall preach;
New creeds and free religions
Self-made apostles teach.

'The peasants to their daily tasks
In surly silence fall;
No kindly hospitalities
In farmhouse or in hall.

'No harvest feast at Christmastide
Shall farm or manor hold
Science alone can plenty give,
The only God is gold.

'The homes where love and peace shall dwell
Fierce politics shall vex;
And unsexed woman try to prove
Herself the coarser sex.

'Mechanics in their workshops
Affairs of State decide;
Honour and truth, old-fashioned words,
The noisy mobs deride.

'The statesmen that should rule the realm
Coarse demagogues displace;
The glory of a thousand years
Shall end in foul disgrace.

'The honour of old England
Cotton shall buy and sell,
And hardware manufacturers
Cry, "Peace! Lo! all is well!"

'Trade shall be held the only good,
And gain the sole device;
The statesman's maxim shall be "Peace,
And peace at any price!"

'Her Army and her Navy
Britain shall cast aside;
Soldiers and ships are costly things,
Defence an empty pride.

'The German and the Muscovite
Shall rule the narrow seas;
Old England's flag shall cease to float
In triumph on the breeze.

'The years roll on; old manners change,
Old customs lose their sway;
New fashions rule; the grandsire's garb
Moves ridicule to-day.

'The woodlands where my race has bred,
Upon the axe shall yield;
Hedgerow and copse shall cease to shade
The ever-widening field.

'The furze down, the moorland heath,
The steam plough shall invade,
Nor park, nor manor shall escape
Common, nor forest glade.

'The manly sports of England
Shall perish one by one;
The manly blood of England
In weaker veins shall run.

'Degenerate sons of manlier sires
To lower joys shall fall;
The faithless lore of Germany,
The gilded vice of Gaul.

'The sports of their forefathers
To baser tastes shall yield,
The vices of the town displace
The pleasures of the field!

'For swiftly o'er the level shore
The waves of progress ride;
The ancient landmarks, one by one,
Shall sink beneath the tide.

'Time-honoured creeds and ancient faith,
The Altar and the Crown
Lordship, hereditary right,
Before that tide go down.

'Base churls shall mock the mighty names
Writ on the roll of time;
Religion shall be held a jest,
And loyalty a crime!

'No word of prayer, no hymn of praise,
Sound in the village school;
The people's education
Utilitarians rule.

'The footstep of the invader
Then England's shores shall know,
While home-bred traitors give the hand
To England's every foe.

'Disarmed before the foreigner,
The knee she'll humbly bend,
And yield the treasure that she lacked
The wisdom to defend!

'But not for aye – yet once again,
When purged by fire and sword,
The land her freedom shall regain,
To manlier thoughts restored.

'Taught wisdom by disaster,
England shall learn to know
That trade is not the only gain
Heaven gives to man below.

'The greed for gold abated,
The golden calf cast down,
Old England's sons again shall raise
The Altar and the Crown!

'Rejoicing seas shall welcome
Their mistress once again;
Again the banner of St. George
Shall rule upon the main!

'The blood of the invader
Her pastures shall manure
His bones unburied on her fields
For monuments endure!

'Again in hall and homestead
Shall joy and peace be seen,
And smiling children raise again
The maypole on the green!

'Again the hospitable board
Shall groan with Xmas cheer,
And mutual service bind again
The peasant and the peer!

'Again the smiling hedgerow
Shall field from field divide;
Again among the woodlands
The scarlet troop shall ride.'

D.W. Nash, *The Fox's Prophecy:
An Episode of the Berkeley Hunt
(Part II)* (1880)

THE ORIGIN OF FOXHUNTING

❖

. . . Foxhunting is an amusement almost exclusively confined to this nation. To identify the precise period when it was first conducted according to the prevailing system of the present century, would be an impossibility, and indeed it is quite evident that it has undergone many gradations and changes. . .

Whatever period we select to investigate the manners, customs, and occupations of the human race, we find that hunting has formed a prominent and interesting portion of their engagements. There are two conspicuous causes from which the origin of the chase may be traced – one, for the purpose of procuring food; the other, that of destroying ferocious or noxious beasts.

The fox is the only one remaining in Great Britain originally included in the latter category; a classification in which it is scarcely consistent to retain him, now that the pursuit of that animal has become one of our principal and most popular national amusements. Hunting is not confined to the civilised portion of mankind; it still continues to be the engagement of the uncultivated savage, as a means of obtaining sustenance.

It is a fact worthy of remark, which we derive from ancient history, that as the prosperity of any country has increased, gymnastic exercises and sporting enterprises have flourished; and whenever they were abandoned, luxury, idleness, and debauchery obtained a footing. As evidence of the great estimation in which he held field sports, Alexander the Great commanded the renowned Aristotle to write a treatise on the subject, for which he was compensated with a large sum of money from the treasury. During the reign of the Emperor Severus, who built the Picts Wall in England, Appianus wrote four books on hunting.

Grotius studied the same subject, more intimately connected with the sport of coursing. Nemesianus, likewise, wrote some poems on hunting, and many other classic authors devoted their talents and labours to a similar purpose.

That our manly sports have been considered worthy the pens of the most able writers of their respective ages, cannot be refuted; and their appreciations must be received as evidence of the importance with which these sports were regarded.

The manner of conducting field sports has varied very considerably at different periods, not only with reference to the customs which have been observed in the pursuit of animals of the same kind, but, taking into account the great numbers which in the feudal ages infested our wilds and forests, and the essential differences in the habits of those creatures, it was evidently imperative to approach and pursue them with various stratagems.

The sturdy bristly boar and ferocious wolf could not be secured on the same terms as the fleet and bounding deer, or the more cautious, timid hare. Hunting was an expression evidently not confined to the pursuit of any particular animals; every creature, from the active squirrel to the sullen wild boar, was, if found in the woods, considered a suitable subject for exercising the talent and feeding the passion – *amor venandi* – of the hunter.

The term hunting in those days took a wide range; for it was used to signify the pursuit and destruction, by any means that could be devised, of any of the wild natives of the woods calculated for food, or of the ferocious ones whose presence was dangerous and annoying. But the word in its present acceptation is confined to chasing animals with hounds.

'Cecil', *Records of the Chase* (1850)

'Old Tom Towler', an elderly huntsman illustrated by the Cockney artist John Leech for Surtees' Mr Sponge's Sporting Tour published in 1853. Leech's genius was to interpret as well as enhance Surtees' great satirical novels.

HUNTING THE FOX

❖

Hunting, like the drama or any other institution, depends for its existence on the support of public opinion.

. . . . . .

Fox-hunting will surely survive from its own innate qualities. The manner in which it has lived through all the obstacles of wartime is a sufficient testimony of its vitality.

Let us not forget that foxes were once hunted and killed in Mayfair and Kensington and that hunting did not cease in the British Isles because Lord Berkeley was no longer able to kennel his hounds at Charing Cross. For every pack that was disestablished by the expansion of cities, others were formed in rural districts, until we now have more packs of Foxhounds in the United Kingdom than we ever had before.

There remains one cardinal principle with regard to the spirit of fox-hunting. If it is to retain its vigour, it must never become the privilege of any particular class. Like all other really good things it is either national or else it is nothing. If ever it presents the appearance of being based on exclusiveness the whole fabric will dissolve. The proper preservation of fox-hunting is a trust held by all parties to its direction, whether landowners, farmers or subscribers in order to provide the healthiest form of British sport for everyone who can enjoy it, whether on foot or on horseback. Hunting is the one field sport left in these islands that in the face of modern luxury still calls for courage, endurance, decision and nerve. Let us hand it down to those who come after us in its best and purest form.

Lord Willoughby de Broke MFH, *Hunting the Fox* (1926)

HUNTING COUNTRIES

ON ENGLAND

⸻ ❖ ⸻

To me, England is the country, and the country is England. And when I ask myself what I mean by England, when I think of England when I am abroad, England comes to me through my various senses – through the ear, through the eye, and through certain imperishable scents. I will tell you what they are, and there may be those among you who feel as I do.

The sounds of England, the tinkle of the hammer on the anvil in the country smithy, the corncrake on a dewy morning, the sound of the scythe against the whetstone, and the sight of a plough team coming over the brow of a hill, the sight that has been seen in England since England was a land, and may be seen in England long after the Empire has perished and every works in England has ceased to function, for centuries the one eternal sight of England.

The wild anemones in the woods in April, the last load at night of hay being drawn down a lane as the twilight comes on, when you can scarcely distinguish the figures of the horses as they take it home to the farm, and above all, most subtle, most penetrating and most moving, the smell of wood smoke coming up in an autumn evening, or the smell of the scutch fires: that wood smoke that our ancestors, tens of thousands of years ago, must have caught on the air when they were coming home with the result of the day's forage, when they were still nomads, and when they were still roaming the forests and the plains of the continent of Europe.

These things strike down into the very depths of our nature, and touch chords – that go back to the beginning of time and the human race, but they are chords that with every year of our life sound a deeper note in our innermost being.

These are the things that make England, and I grieve for it that they are not the childish inheritance of the majority of the people today in our country. They ought to be the inheritance of every child born into this country, but nothing can be more touching than to see how the working man and woman after generations in the towns will have their tiny bit of garden if they can, will go to gardens if they can, to look at something they have never seen as children, but which their ancestors knew and loved. The love of these things is innate and inherent in our people. It makes for that love of home, one of the strongest features of our race, and it is that that makes our race seek its new home in the Dominions overseas, where they have room to see things like this that they can no more see at home. It is that power of making homes, almost peculiar to our people, and it is one of the sources of their greatness.

They go overseas, and they take with them what they learned at home: love of justice, love of truth, and the broad humanity that are so characteristic of English people.

It may well be that these traits on which we pride ourselves, which we hope to show and try to show in our own lives, may survive – survive among our people so long as they are a people

'The Blackmore and Sparkford Vale', 1980, by John King. He is a leading contemporary sporting artist whose work often derives from close observation through hunting with many packs. The Blackmore and Sparkford Vale pack are depicted running from Inwood. This picture was presented to Tony Austin on resigning the Mastership.

– and I hope and believe this, that just as today, more than fifteen centuries since the last of those great Roman legionaries left England, we still speak of the Roman strength, and the Roman work, and the Roman character, so perhaps in the ten thousandth century, long after the Empires of this world as we know them have fallen and others have risen and fallen, and risen and fallen again, the men who are then on this earth may yet speak of those characteristics which we prize as the characteristics of the English, and that long after, maybe, the name of the country has passed away, wherever men are honourable and upright and persevering, lovers of home, of their brethren, of justice and of humanity, the men in the world of that day may say, 'We still have among us the gifts of that great English race'.

Earl Baldwin of Bewdley, *Speech at annual dinner of the Royal Society of St George*, 6 May, 1924

FOXHUNTING
IN HAMPSHIRE, BERKSHIRE AND WILTSHIRE

❖

Urbanisation, busy roads, railway lines and serious shooting are amongst the problem the masters have to cope with in this area. However, there are still some marvellous wild pockets where real good sport can be enjoyed. In many countries, shooting has gone hand-in-hand with the foxhunting for more than a century, and the cooperation is outstanding. Good communications and a high population, in the main, bring a large following, both mounted and on foot, and the economics, in spite of a difficult climate, are sound and consequently standards are maintained. As with most things in life the more you put in, the more you can take out – hunting is no exception and enthusiasm and dedication can still produce sparkling sport on restricted pitches.

Taking the countries of the area alphabetically, the Avon Vale has a strongly fenced, good scenting grass vale, but the country is interspersed with numerous towns. However, they have a great tradition of sporting farmers who make the hounds very welcome. George Hyatt, previously Master of the South Devon and Huntsman of the Curre and the Tipperary, is the professional Huntsman. He has a great reputation across the country, having been a prominent point-to-point rider and he produces good sport for the thrusters.

The Garth and South Berks is one of several celebrated packs near London which have amalgamated. The M4 runs through the country, but Ian Langrish, in his 25th season as Huntsman, knows the difficulties well. There are many large woodlands, which ride deep but carry a scent. They are a particularly good looking pack of hounds, going back to those of Colonel Rodney Palmer. The Colonel was a brother-in-law of the late Sir Peter Farquhar and had access to the very best blood. Mr Bob Phillips carried on the lines during his Mastership and the present breeders have a very sound base to build on.

The HH (Hampshire Hunt) is a well-run country and probably the best supported in the area. A very strong Mastership is headed by Mr John Gray, who farms widely and is a leading figure in the countryside – he is in his 30th season. Hopper Cavendish is a top class hunter judge and takes charge of the hound breeding, while Mr Andreae is a landowner whose family have been involved over many years. The country has large woodlands, but the open areas are well provided with jumping places. There are some very good shoots, but first class cooperation exists between the two sports, which has been built up by diplomatic Masters and huntsmen over a long period. Bob Collins is the enthusiastic and popular Huntsman. His

'The Duke of Beaufort's – Gone Away from Tog Hill', 1960, by Michael Lyne. The US sporting art collector Paul Mellon is in the foreground riding his hunter Enough Rope.

brother is at the Seavington, while another brother is a gamekeeper. They spring from a Somerset family of sporting farmers.

The Hursley Hambledon perhaps has more problems than its neighbour, but the Huntsman, Douglas Hunt, is in his 30th season, having started under the celebrated Colonel Frank Mitchell. Mr and Mrs Peter Humphrey, who have large agricultural business interests locally, have been Senior Masters for 12 seasons, and Mrs Humphrey takes great trouble both in the country and breeding the hounds. There is some lovely open downland to the west of the kennels at Droxford, and this experienced team produces a lot of fun.

The Isle of Wight has little trouble with invasion by its neighbours, but does have a very strong local following. There are plenty of thick, good, holding gorses, interspersed with rolling, galloping country, while there is some intensive vegetable protection on the low ground. Mr Michael Poland, after a long spell as Master of the Hambledon, where he still resides, has been Master for 12 seasons. A studious and successful hound breeder, he has recently also turned his attention to the turf, and bred and half-owned Kings Theatre, only just beaten in the 1994 epic Derby and winner of the George VI Diamond Stakes at Ascot. Henry Cecil has judged at the Puppy Show, which is a particularly hospitable event, with many visitors from the mainland being entertained by Mr and Mrs Poland, and his Huntsman, Giles Wheeler, who previously whipped-in at Badminton.

The New Forest hounds are hunted by the writer, but thanks to Sir Newton Rycroft's breeding, they are a good working pack with an above-average cry, which is useful in the Forest. The country is 60 per cent woodland and the remainder open heath, with bogs and plenty of heather, bracken and gorse, and also people! There are over nine million visitors a year, but the area is hunted by the foxhounds, the buckhounds, and the beagles. With careful organisation and great cooperation from the authorities it is still a fine country to see and hear the hounds. Being very good scenting, all three packs run at a good pace. There are plenty of hirelings and visitors are very welcome.

The Royal Artillery are enjoying a very successful time. Colonel John Jago had nine good seasons, and the new Master, Major Jonathon Seed, showed splendid sport last season. The hunting is mainly on Salisbury Plain, with plenty of opportunities to see the hounds without too much inconvenience from having to jump. However, the Plain produces its own hazards and a handy horse is desirable. Support for this pack has increased of late and there are often over 60 riders out.

The Tedworth are fortunate to have the services of Captain Rupert Inglesant as Master and Huntsman. His father was a distinguished Secretary of the Quorn Hounds and Rupert is an accomplished race rider. David Jukes, ex-Huntsman of the Zetland, is Kennel Huntsman and lst Whipper-In. The country is mainly arable, with some downland and plenty of shooting. The present incumbents have produced good sport, and morale in the country is extremely high.

The Vine and Craven are hunted by Mr Richard Hill, who formerly hunted the Spooners and West Dartmoor – quite a contrast. He has the assistance of Mr Robin Mackenzie as Joint Master, whose local knowledge and public relations skills must be invaluable. It is, for the main part, light galloping downland with some fine country about Kingsclere. The racing community are very supportive.

'The Portman', by John King. Hounds and horses are seen washing off at Manston, Stour Valley, North Dorset, after a busy day in the deep-riding, strongly fenced Saturday Vale.

The Wilton are enjoying a 'golden age'. Mr James Bouskell, a keen shooting man, gained the confidence and support of the shooting community during his Mastership 1983–1991, and created a first rate organisation. To the delight of everyone, he has rejoined the Mastership; meanwhile his wife is also Master and has bred a good pack. Lady Traill, an elegant former Lady Mayoress of London, completes a Mastership of the highest quality. Peter Barker is well established as professional Huntsman and, although this is a cold scenting chalk down country, he gets his hounds to run well. The country is very well jumped.

The South and West Wilts is a very large country with tremendous variety, stretching from Salisbury Plain, over the Wiltshire Downs, to the Knoyle Vale on the east end of the Blackmore Vale, with some big Somerset woodlands and the very deep Witham Vale to the north-west. David Herring, a very experienced Master and Huntsman, is in charge. There are no large towns and plenty of elbow room, and fields tend to be small. Both vales are strongly fenced and need a bold horse with stamina. The lines created by Ikey Bell flow strongly through the blood of the present pack, who take some keeping with when the vale or downs are wet.

Simon Clarke, Master and Huntsman of the New Forest, previously hunted the South Dorset, the Cottesmore, the Duke of Buccleuch's and the South and West Wilts.

Simon Clarke, *Baily's Hunting Companion* (1994)

THE SHIRES –
AN AUTUMN GALLOP
WITH THE QUORN

❖

The last Friday in October was signalised by as fast and cheery a gallop as is likely to mark the Quorn season '83–'84. Thirty flying minutes from Gaddesby Spinney over some of the prettiest ground of the Hunt, and with just enough people for the requirements of good-fellowship.

A hundred might have ridden to hounds without getting in each other's way – so fair, open, and roomy was the country of today. I would put you in the middle of the scurry forthwith, and send you cramming and spurring in pursuit of those lithesome ladies at once but that every tale must have its beginning, its characters however few, its events however tamed by fact, and its sequel however ordinary. Wherever you have been of late, you know of the soft misty days that characterised the latter half of October. The Friday in question was a full example – drizzly and almost chilly as one stood still; wet, hot, and choking as one galloped and jumped. A few people had been at Ashby Pastures when hounds were cast into it at ten o'clock; a good many more had turned up at their leisure during the morning while hounds were fighting against a weak scent among falling leaves in covert, and doing their best and liveliest against short-running foxes outside.

Gaddesby Spinney is a little copse, with the name of which my kindly readers must be only too familiar, for does it not recur as regularly and almost as profusely, autumn after autumn, as the falling of the leaf?

Distinct among Mr Cheney's other and equally valued patches of covert in the neighbourhood, the plantation that lies about half a mile westward of the village retains the denomination. And some thirty individuals, all darkly dressed and dripping, clustered at its edge in the early afternoon of Friday.

The old sweet sound! *Hark* to it, old ladies! The covert's a tiny one; a fox is a fact, a scent is more than likely, and a gallop ought to be a certainty.

Out flashes the fact – No! Tally-ho, back! and may Tom Moody's ghost haunt the fool on foot at the corner!

Ah, but that slip back was only a ruse; already they are screaming away at the end of the covert opposite the village; and now you may kick-in-and-out of the rough ridge-and-furrow as fast as you can.

By virtue of habit, the timekeepers dive at their fobs. 'One-thirty by my old clock, anything you like by the time-but help me remember one-thirty.'

'A moment, ONE moment, please, gentlemen!'– and the ladies come bundling out among and behind the little throng that has whisked all too hastily round to the holloa. Twenty yards from the covert is a tall thorn fence still bearing, in gorgeous red and faded green, the full foliage of summer.

In a second or two every hound has dived nosily through the gaudy screen; and the music moves lustily on – but whither the pack may be pointing is a matter of vaguest guess. The lengthy and impenetrable curtain must be outflanked one way or the other.

Please yourself whether you gallop back or gallop on.

Choosing onward, you will reach the Gaddesby Road, and cut off the pack if it bends to the right. Slip back and you make it safe should it turn to the left. Firr, with a trusting majority after him, takes the latter course. Supposing for once you are misguided enough to put more faith in your own instinct than in that of the huntsman, you soon find yourself hammering the road, with the invisible chorus gradually waxing fainter – while the stroke of your gallop and the beat of your own heart grow faster and faster. Leftward they've turned, by all that's brief in life and deceptive in hope! Easy enough – and often convenient enough – it is to get into a broad road; but to leave it (as pulpit and experience have taught us all our lives) is a very different task.

So for a long quarter of a mile never an outlet presents itself. A gate at last – and off to the left the gleam of a white hound darting through the second fence away.

Those two fences and two great furrowed fields are made up as quickly as hot anxiety and a big striding horse can manage. In the third, the two streams reunite; and we are galloping in the train of the huntsman's party.

Amid these light little meadows and their thick leafy hedges you will see nothing of hounds unless you are on their backs. But the single redcoat is the best of beacons, as it flickers brightly over each intervening barrier, or flashes like a meteor across some rising ground.

This may help you to cut into the grassy lane of the Gaddesby and Brooksby bridle road, and to catch the swinging hand-gate that opens into the wide Brooksby pastures – while Mr Alfred Brocklehurst, on the best of timber-jumpers, launches over the rails by the side, and the voice of the less venturesome pleads, 'Do as you would be done by, and keep it open for me'.

Twenty couple, young and old, are driving down the wide green slope – the old ladies straining madly on the ravishing scent, the youngsters catching the new excitement that they had never felt to the full before.

We ought to know this bridle path, and should have learned to open its easy gates ere now. But the three leaders find no time nor need to stop – so why should reader and I?

The fence in the valley is but a flying trifle; though little clue can we gather of its make and width till we see that Mr H. T. Barclay is safely landed – and we wonder why his horse should have taken no note of the grass-grown rivulet beyond, which ours emphasized with so pronounced a peck on his knees and nose.

Up the brow the next is a fair, pleasant jump, and so is the following one. But 'Ware wire!' sends a chill down our backbone as we approach the third – and right gladly do we mark the pack turning along the dreaded barrier. At this time of year above all others is wire our phantom, too often our embodied, enemy.

Not only is the light-stretched strand far more difficult to perceive through the leafy branches of October, but the fat stock has not yet found a market, and the farmers are loth to weaken their fences too soon.

Year by year, however, we gladly and thankfully notice a diminution, even during the summer, in the quantity of wire set to guard the fences of the Midlands. It is found to be so fruitful of injury to cattle, so easily knocked out of order, and withal so indifferent a protection against the bull-headed pertinacity of a restless shorthorn, that its apparent economy is no longer a recommendation, and very few lines of wire fencing are now either fresh set or renewed. Soon may the old-fashioned oxer again reign paramount, to invite or repel with its rugged honesty – according to the measure and prompting of our years, (a pun would be a vile thing even in the cause of pusillanimity) and our discretion. But the wire in question stretches only half the breadth of the field; and with the regard for their followers that so constantly characterized the movements of fox and hounds throughout this merry gallop, they now strike through the hedge almost exactly where the metal ends – and while we behind gasp 'Wire!' they in front charge a hole in the fence, and sweep down the wide stretching pasture in full content.

Many a gallop have I ridden in Leicestershire (as I e'en hope to do again) – and have seen hounds and horses go away from me more often than I should like to say – but never has the pace seemed better than now.

Fast horses are galloping their utmost on the fairest turf, an easy fence comes perhaps in half a mile of galloping, gates are either standing open, or fly back at once to the crop – and yet the pack is going all too fast for us unwilling laggards, till a wandering shepherd throws a chance turn in our favour.

Now we cross the Melton and Leicester turnpike, midway between Rearsby and Brooksby; now we have worked through a few pumping acres of newly turned arable, and now we are pushing up the big grass field for the covert of Bleakmore, marvelling why the turf seems less elastic, and the stride of our horse less conformable with ridge and furrow, than only a few brief minutes ago.

Yes, lungs and muscle are never in autumn what they may be after Xmas – and 'tis only the commencement of the lesson yet.

Fondly we hug ourselves that Bleakmore is just in front; and that in another minute we shall be on foot beside our fat steeds – mopping our foreheads with gusto, and flinging our tongues in noisy exuberant accord on the subject of the pleasant scurry just over.

Not yet.

For the merry ladies race onwards along the ridge – leaving Bleakmore and the railway below them on the right.

How now for your 'honest oxer'? Here it is in its most laudable ruggedness – and, in plain Saxon, an ugly beast it is too.

The rail on the take-off side is no excuse for the qualm that stabs you like the conscience of

'The Burton', by John King. Dating back to 1672, the Burton in North Lincolnshire, is one of the oldest Hunts. It is heavily ploughed, but well drained with deep dykes as illustrated here.

a schoolboy caught cribbing his task. But the high laid-fence shows its strong teeth e'en through the heavy foliage; a ditch of unknown dimensions lies beyond; there is a whisper, too, of wire; and any number of predecessors are not likely to bring things to a much lower level.

The huntsman quickly makes up his mind to the inevitable; but his horse (brilliantly as he carries him throughout) on this occasion whips round to take time for a second thought.

Mr Brocklehurst clears the whole difficulty a few yards to the right, while the Cambridgeshire hero takes the office from Firr, and makes a bold bid for victory. Post and rails, hedge and ditch are covered gallantly. But beyond them all, and visible only from mid-air, glistens another stout ox rail.

'Forty to one against Bendigo!' shouts his familiar friend as he himself lands in safety.

But the only response to the liberal offer is a loud cracking of timber, a heavy flounder and another good man fallen on the turf. Matters are a little simpler now; and after seeing the huntsman, Captain O'Neal, Mr Peake, Mr Cradock, Mr Alston, and two or three others, surmount the less complicated difficulty, reader and I too may pull ourselves together, put our panting beast through the same process – by help of knee and heel against his well-furnished sides – and even reach the others as, after another half-mile of grass, they muddle at a bridle gate by Rearsby.

The fox had swung to the left, again across the turnpike; but with such a scent as there is today, the pack falters neither on road nor plough, but drives forward over the little fields behind the village, whether they happen to be eddish or arable.

Scarcely so with their followers. The drive is wellnigh spent, the steel is out of the iron, and the oil is all but burned out. A horse will gallop in a mechanical sort of way, long after the power to jump has left him. A very limited experience with the symptoms suffices to teach us where such a stage has been reached; also that a mere mechanical stride is of little use against a strong top binder.

It by no means follows that the faculty of appreciation adds greatly to our enjoyment at such moments.

I confess to its having a very contrary effect upon my frail nerves – and I venture to assert, by the way, that the one great drawback to the pleasures of steeplechase jockeyship lies in the frequent necessity of riding a beaten horse home. Now, however, there are gates and gaps to help us.

Again we are on the grass, and at the pace hounds are running they must surely catch a view in another minute or two.

A shepherd – with more than the acumen or consideration of his race, holding his collie in his arms – declares 'the fox is nobbut a hoondred ya-ards afore 'em!' the while he fumbles at an unwilling gate, and we pant and ejaculate, and hope there is no more hunting to be done.

'Forrard, little bitches,' rings cherrily out as the pack glides up the hedge-side, and we follow hurriedly to the corner – trusting that, as hitherto, Providence and enlightened agriculture will have provided free means of egress from field to field.

Yes, there's a nice stile for the use of labourers and for people on foot – and well used it evidently is, for the approach to it is worn into a hole, and slimy clay has taken the place of grass. Beyond this, the corner is a veritable cul de sac; for lofty bullfinches of an earlier generation enclose either flank – and despair settles upon our souls.

If you, reader, happen to have hunted in the Pytchley country some twenty years ago, when that flying huntsman, and most rapid yet laconic of talkers, Charles Pain, was in his prime, you may remember an oft-quoted incident that eminently illustrated the man.

Reaching a certain corner, from which the only apparent escape was retreat – (the last alternative that ever occurred to his mind) he found another hard rider just turning reluctantly away.

Charles Pain was one who suited his words to his actions, the latter being quite as rapid and ready as the former – so, taking his horse short by the head, he pursued his way without further ado, accompanying and explaining his progress only with a single running sentence, 'Will do,

'The Cotswold – Lawn Meet at Sudgrove House', 1975, oil painting by Michael Lyne. Pat and Sam Koechlin-Smythe are seen bringing refreshments to the Hunt.

will do – must do, must do; d–d woolly place – hold up ye beggar – hey bitch!' Men who knew him in those days will easily fill in for themselves the rapidity of his jerky utterances, and the high treble pitch to which the last syllable would raise him.

Alas for the feelings of him who had turned aside; alas for the plight of those who would ride to his lead! Think you they found their situation any more palatable than ours now – Firr's whitelegged bay having shown us all a clean pair of heels – our fox said to be dead beat, and our horses undoubtedly so?

Well, must do, must do – and Kismet is kind to the next three – too kind, for they do nothing to mend matters for those who have yet to come. No. 4 has already declared loudly that he cannot, nay, that he *will* not; for that

> The heart of his good horse
> Was nigh to burst with violence of the beat,
> And so perforce he stayed, and overtaken spoke.

But finding himself, like a bull in a pound, and that neither Tennyson nor any other man is likely to help him out, unless he helps himself, he too puts his head down and goes for the opening – if so it might be called.

It has every claim to the title when he has done with it; for half a ton of beaten horse-flesh will splinter almost any top-bar in the country, that has been rained upon for more than a single year, (and this is one of the reasons for our constant assertion that big horses are better than little ones, to carry us in Leicestershire).

That such a result, however, cannot always be attained without a certain concussion was, he tells me, instanced in the query of his groom that night – 'Wasn't it close at home as you fell, sir? I thought as the colour of the dirt on the chesnut's head looked as if it were.'

Meanwhile the hounds have encountered their first momentary check – their fox having been driven almost back among them by two men who shouted in his very face.

But for this they must have pulled him down in a few more fields. Now they of course flash beyond the point; recover themselves, however, and the line very quickly; but lose a very vital half-minute.

By this time the circle is nearly completed, and the boundary brook between the Gaddesby and Brooksby parishes is reached where rails must be born down, while hounds go on alone.

Again we are on the Brooksby manor; again hounds are going faster than we can, and we are going very much faster than our horses.

Indeed, as WHO-HOOP sounds over a drain, at the road immediately above the hall, only the Master and his man are there at the moment to give it – 'the field in varied plight arriving as best they can.' We shall see nothing faster, and we may see very few things better this year. I have made a long story of these thirty minutes.

Captain E. Pennell Elmhirst ('Brooksby') *The Best Season on Record* (1884)

WITH THE PUCKERIDGE AND THURLOW

❖

The fog was thick when the Puckeridge and Thurlow hounds met at Walsall Green on November 29th, 1975. With a large field I decided to hunt even so; a risk which led to a memorable hunt. After drawing some artichokes by Furneux Pelham and Rogers Wood, hounds picked up the stale line of a fox above Boxens Green and rather hesitantly headed for Hormead Park.

Mrs Vestey and her two elder sons, hotfoot from Eton on St Andrew's Day, then loomed out of the clearing fog with news of a fox on the move that they had met a few minutes earlier while trying to find hounds. That lucky encounter was really the start of the day.

I lifted hounds and they were soon away very fast to Patrick's Wood, where deer caused a slight diversion. Hounds retrieved the line and ran on past Brent Pelham, almost to the kennels, and swung left-handed through the Dairy to Cole Green. A short check, before Mrs Streeter spotted the fox going away to Meesden Hall, where he bemused some pigs, but without delay they took the line out to Further Ford End. Here Virgin, a pure English Hound, put them right, across the Stort, and they then ran past Ruttels to Clavering Place, through Wood Hall, Severals, Wicken Osiers and Whiteditch Farm, to Wenden's Ambo.

Left-handed just short of the village, they hunted nicely back towards Arkesden, where Mr Ted Harvey viewed the fox not far ahead. By this time Ron Quarmby was hunting Hounds as I had been badly baulked by wire by Clavering Place.

A long check by Severals, complicated by a stag, and then some shooters put us right when they spotted our fox, who had lain down, pick himself up out of the middle of a stubble field. Retracing his steps, the fox ran through Wood Hall, past Clavering Place, Valence, Roast Green, Further Ford End, to Meesden Hall Wood, where he did a circuit and then decided to take refuge under a pile of logs in Mrs Tyler's garden where he had to be left. Hounds first picked up the line at 12.30. They put him to ground in the dusk at 4.15. An eight mile point. Nineteen miles at least as they ran, with only two grass fields from start to finish, and on neither of these could hounds really hunt. Starting with a field of 90, seven saw the end; Mr and Mrs Vestey and their sons Timothy and James, Mr Pat Lloyd, my daughter, Diana Pyper, and Mr Christopher Sporberg, the field master. A marvellous plough country hunt, with several of the progeny of the Duke of Beaufort's Beadle '66 prominent throughout.

Captain Charles Barclay MFH, *Great Days* (1997)

THE PORTMAN

❖

Seldom is optimism repaid as quickly as occurred after my wish last week for improved scent and longer points.

My Christmas Eve hunt was one of the most enjoyable I can ever remember in the festive season, thanks to both the elements of the Chase so devoutly wished for being present in full measure.

Since the local correspondent, Ballyn Garry, has been somewhat dilatory this season, he kindly allowed me to record the hunt in question, achieved by the Portman hounds in their deep, grass vale which lies below Bulbarrow Hill. This area of North Dorset, smallish dairy farms below and broad downlands above, with occasional secret places in tree clad coombes, has a touch of wildness and even mystery about it which makes it a delight to explore at any time, but never better than when following hounds.

Hunting history abounds: more than 2,000 years ago the pre-Roman iron age settlers hunted from their hill forts of which traces remain at Rawlsbury where Portman foxes so often run; and in the late 18th century Peter Beckford, who wrote *Thoughts on Hunting*, followed his hounds in these North Dorset hills and valleys. From his observations was born one of the classics on the noble science of venery.

We enjoyed the warm hospitality of Mr Martin Mayne at Chitcombe House, Woolland, on Christmas Eve, and almost inevitably our first fox soon took hounds up the steep slopes of Bulbarrow Hill, behind Woolland. As you ride after them, hounds look like seagulls wheeling against a green sky, but most of your attention is needed to nurse your panting horse up the 900 ft slope.

This was a short-lived hunt, however, and soon we were following hounds in the vale again, as they drew the formidable, wide hedges set on banks which harbour foxes as frequently as the coverts. The natural obstacles to be jumped in this vale can never be trifled with, since even the most innocent looking flyer may easily hide a yarning ditch and a big drop. The growth is too thick to permit them to be banked, and the horse which takes liberties with width or height soon pays for it with a fall.

Joint-Master Mr John Woodhouse, who has also been the Portman's Hon. Secretary for 21 years, holloaed away the fox which provided the day's major hunt. He saw it in Whitecombe Lane after hounds spoke on Mr Frank Kent's farm at Stoke Wake. Huntsman Geoffrey Harrison had the pack nicely together on what proved to be an excellent line, with a fast improving scent.

They ran towards Droop, swinging left-handed to Park Gate, back across Mr Kent's farm and over Stoke Common. Then it was puff and pull again for the horses as we ascended Bulbarrow's neighbour, White Hill, but there were smiles all round as the fox sank the vale

'The South Shropshire': by the renowned sporting photographer Jim Meads from his book My Hunting World (Quiller Press). Huntsman Michael Rowson is seen at Lyth Hill, near Church Stretton, collecting his hounds at the end of a morning's cubhunting.

again, running by Rawlsbury Wood and over the Ansty-Mappowder road into the neighbouring South Dorset country.

Our fox pressed on down the vale, crossing Hatherly Dairy Farm, and skirting Melcombe Park to run through Humber Wood. Here, two and a half couple remained, marking at a drain under a gate, but the main body moved on quickly and there is every reason to believe they did not change.

The line continued across the Mappowder-Plush road, then going through Ball Copse on to Ball Wood, swinging left-handed round the back of the Old Fox Inn Folly, and crossing the valley bottom before ascending Lyscombe Hill. Here, the few remaining mounted followers were cheered on by two gentlemen on foot who proved to be the Joint-Master and huntsman of the South Dorset Hunt, Mr Alastair Jackson, and fellow Joint-Master, Mr Edgar Tory. They watched our sport with the extra benevolence of those who had just enjoyed a seven-mile point with their own hounds.

Fortunately for the horses, in view of the 'mountaineering' now required, the pace decreased considerably, but the Portman hounds continued to make the line across Lyscombe Bottom, up over Hog Hill and the stretch of arable land beyond the Cheselbourne-Piddletrenthide road, where the fox had to be given best in darkness at Kingcombe. It had been a five-mile point, with hounds running more than twice the distance, in less than 90 minutes.

Just as in the great days when J. J. Farquharson hunted most of Dorset in the last century, one of the chief joys of this sort of line was the wonderful variety of terrain, almost entirely on grass, but changing from deep riding vale, and stiff fences, to narrow tracks through woodland, to soaring hills with wide expanses of grass.

Of the dozen or so who finished I especially noted young Charlie Gordon-Watson, riding his brilliant grey pony, Shade – both rider and mount aged 14 – formerly ridden by his elder sister, the Olympic gold medallist, Mary Gordon-Watson, who earlier this season brought Cornishman out with the Portman. Their father, Brig. Gordon-Watson, was also one of those who finished this enjoyable hunt.

Jogging through several of the vale's little villages, guided by cheerful lights beneath their low-thatched roofs, it was indeed worth rejoicing that we would soon be changing to a New Year bearing ample proof that some of the countryside's traditional pleasures remain as enduring as ever – offering so many more pleasures in the year ahead.

Michael Clayton ('Foxford') *Foxhunting Companion* (1978)

THE COLLEGE VALLEY

❖

Foxhunting in the College Valley's country in the Cheviots fortunately involves few problems – and the rewards far outweigh them.

In a testing country for hounds, it goes without saying that the problems are minimised if hounds start hunting in the best condition and as fit as possible. The degree of supervision which can be exercised once cubhunting commences is limited by the roughness of the country. The schooling of hounds on the roads and in the fields to ensure they have an eye for the movements of their huntsman, and that they meet and resist the temptations on exercise that they will later have to ignore in the field, is therefore all the more important.

There can be no holding up of cubs on the hill, and the problem is to locate the litter of cubs before an old fox decides to step in and draw hounds away. A big bracken bed is ideal cover to start hounds off in. It should be thick enough to provide ample shield for the foxes and to keep hounds 'on their noses,' but not so thick as to allow hounds from working up close to their quarry more quickly than they would in thick brambles or patches of gorse.

On a bad scenting morning the hill huntsman has to be patient, for he could soon bottom a half fit horse attempting to help his hounds out of their difficulties. The remedies are all too plain to see from a vantage point, but intervention is best preserved for the right moment in the closing stages of the hunt when the fox is beginning to tire.

On a good scenting morning, hounds require little help and the main problem is to stop them hunting before the young entry and the horses have had enough! The hills, of course, afford the huntsman great opportunity to study which hounds are doing the work, especially during cubhunting when they run locally and are seldom out of view, and there can be no finer backcloth for a pack than a hillside with the varied tones of bracken, heather and moss on a bright October morning.

Foxes often run far in October – probably as families and cubs are splitting up and some are driven far afield by parents who feel they have done their stint, and by hostile neighbours. A seven mile point is the longest we have secured in this month recently.

In November the bracken goes down and foxes have to fly, though increasing afforestation and growth of gorse in the valley bottoms provides much extra cover in the country than there was 10 years ago. The good hill fox lies out in most weather, on the screes on a sunny day or in deep heather on the tops.

He is easily disturbed and is usually on his legs well before hounds draw up to him. He never waits for hounds and if they 'fresh find' it is invariably a fresh fox.

Hill foxes are well aware of the advantages of running through sheep, and the Cheviot Hills are much more heavily stocked than most other hill countries, such as the Fells. There is no more graceful sight than a fox running a wall, and they do this often, and when hard hunted often turn over the steepest of going to gain time, or run the stones by the riversides where scent lies badly.

Lack of cover is, of course, the problem for a tiring fox in a hill country and they often tuck themselves away into farm buildings. One of our shepherds got the fright of his life (and lost a pailful of milk in the process) when a fox, hard hunted in the morning, decided at dusk that it was safe to move from his refuge among the hay bales in the byre – and almost landed on the back of a cow as it was being milked!

Terrier work is an essential part of hunting in the hills, for the more foxes you catch the more you have the following year. Shepherds and volunteers put to the largest holes and of course where soil is shallow so are the holes, so digging is not always a lengthy business.

A more skilful pen than mine has described the type of hound Sir Alfred Goodson has bred to hunt the country. Perseverance is a quality that has not, perhaps, received sufficient mention, for a hill hound must try for his fox and mark him without the support of his huntsman, who cannot always be to hand in terms of hours rather than minutes.

Independence can be a fault as well as a quality, and the right degree comes only through careful breeding and handling. A good hill hound, with his independence, high spirits and activity, is not the easiest animal to handle, especially in his youth. Yet if his mettle is steered on the right course, he is a most rewarding hound with which to hunt the fox.

In the time I have had the good fortune to hunt the College Valley I have handled no better dog than Raglan ('66). He was the best of a very good litter of four dogs and two bitches, and combined all the qualities of a good working hound. As well as possessing great fox sense, he was an exceptional fox-catcher, his muzzle being like a hard-working terrier by the end of the season.

Raglan had a great end in late March '71. Hounds found a good fox on Langleeford. After a turn into the West Percy country, they climbed out to Cheviot itself, and after 90 minutes and a five mile point, the fox was beat and turned off the hill to be overhauled at Coldburn Rocks.

It would be surprising if Raglan was not closely concerned at the finish but when Mrs Letts arrived first up, he was just able to greet her before dying of heart failure alongside his last fox.

However there are many of his progeny hunting here and elsewhere. A good many of them have his foxcatching ability, and there are few who do not inherit his enthusiasm for the best of all sports – foxhunting.

Martin Letts MFH, *Foxhunting Companion* (1978)

Lord Scamperdale and his 'man' Jack Spraggon hacking in a fog to the cross-roads at Dallington Burn, wood cut by John Leech from Mr Sponge's Sporting Tour.

SOUTH DORSET

❖

Who cares what anyone else thinks, your own hunt, like your own regiment, is the best. But, in sober truth, there really cannot be anything quite to match the little patch of vale, centred on Dungeon Hill, hunted by the South Dorset, with its small field, seldom more than 40, just for three months a year on every other Tuesday. We live slap bang in the middle of it.

When I was a boy we used to bank the hedges; you could get anywhere on a clever pony, up out of the clinging clay over a ditch, scramble somehow through the cut-and-lay, and down ditto. But now that the hedges are cut en brosse, you have to fly the lot or find a gate, only an athletic horse and a good heart will do for the South Dorset Vale today. Old Woody, the best horse I ever owned, who had nerve enough for both of us, is past it now, and so am I, but he was in his prime five years ago.

It was just before Christmas. After a week of fog and frosts the forecast was for a wet, unsettled day. The temperature was west, and the glass steady. Smoke was fleeing chimneys, and heavy clouds dragged their skirts across the downland escarpment to our south as we hacked the four miles to the meet at Mappowder, where we joined the usual vale field, perhaps three dozen, including the lucky handful of visitors who had managed to get round the Secretary.

It was a busy morning, plenty of foxes, scent catchy, but we covered a lot of ground, had some adventures, and everyone was in a happy mood as we hacked back by road to the meet from a three mile point that had taken us into neighbouring country. Second horses were taken, by those few who had them, we are not really that sort of hunt. The temperature had dropped, the promised wind was rising throwing occasional handfuls of rain into our faces, when a hedgerow fox was found, and hounds got off almost on his brush. He took a quick circuit in the vale, and then headed for the hills, hounds giving a wonderful and helpful cry.

The obstacle that immediately faced us was a large hedge by any standards, bringing down three or four of the first who tackled it. In the fraction of doubtful pause that followed I fancied that I heard the hounds well to our left, and running south, in the opposite direction; it is convenient to have such fancies when the way forward is uninviting but just for once, fancy proved correct.

Catching a gate before the stewards shut it, and hopping a few familiar rails, I made Horse Close, 40 acres of bog and woodland, just after hounds had entered it, and was joined by the huntsman and the only two members of the field to survive the imbroglio at the monster hedge. Hounds crashed on, forcing their fox out of cover, up the steep slope of the downland at the vale's edge, and into the wood above, the pace was terrific.

We straggled, the huntsman going on, and we doing our best to help him forward, and seeing to the gates. Suddenly, I'm not sure how, in a place oddly and memorably named

'The Fernie – Away from Bunker's Hill' c. 1963, oil painting by John Kenny. The Fernie's superb Leicestershire country, north of Market Harborough, was originally part of the Quorn country until 1853 when it was hunted separately by the son of the Quorn's Master Sir Richard Sutton. After disputes the Fernie later established its independence.

Bloody Tent Wood, a locked wicket divided Edward Knowles from his hounds, and me from my companion. He climbed the gate, changed horses, and we picked our way gingerly, he and I, down through the wood to where the hounds were by then marking at an enormous badger set. And that is how, completely undeserved, out of a field of nearly forty Woody and I ended a good thing in the South Dorset vale alone with the hounds.

The day was not finished, but we were. The first hard surface discovered a clanking shoe, and I turned for home. A gale was getting up, and the occasional dash of rain suggested such haste as was decent with a tired deserving horse. Five miles to go and the light just failing, it could have been any Christmas holiday evening since childhood. Woody was no doubt thinking of his manger, I was pondering the article I had to write – it had been, by chance, my debut as a hunting correspondent, and the best day I can remember.

David Edelsten, *Great Days* (1997)

'Mr Caingey Thornton doesn't "put on steam enough"' – aftermath of a fall in a brook, by John Leech from Mr Sponge's Sporting Tour.

MIDDLETON

❖

The best day that I can recall, although I was not actually out, was the 12th January 1971 when my father, Lord Halifax, was hunting The Middleton hounds and it was such an exceptional hunt that it is one that I must describe. The start had been delayed owing to a sharp frost, when the bitches met at Westow. Going to Howsham Wood, they found and went away by Gally Gap towards Leppington on by Scrayingham and the Gilder Beck, to the foot of the Wolds above Kirby Underdale.

All this had been at a good pace, but as hounds breasted the Wolds through Noodle, to cross the York to Bridlington Road, they raced on, and it was here that the horses could not keep up. The frost was coming on producing a breast high scent and everyone was struggling to keep in touch. My father, who was hunting hounds, and his kennel huntsman, Dennis Sturgeon, disembarked into vehicles and by hearsay they managed to follow on by Huggate, Millington Pastures to Warter Priory estate, one of the best shoots in Yorkshire.

By then it was dark and, thanks to the keepers there, my father and Dennis were able to collect up the hounds, all of which were on and showing signs of having killed their fox. The next morning, the keepers presented my father with the fox's mask, which proved they had indeed killed their fox.

This was a remarkable hunt over the best of the Middleton country with a 12 mile point. Sir William Brooksbank of Menethorpe, who was then field master, gave my father a detailed map of the hunt, framed as a picture, with the names of all the hounds who were hunting that day on it. Today this still hangs at Garrowby for the present Lord Halifax.

Lady Caroline Gosling, *Great Days* (1997)

THE BORDER

❖

My best day was a meet at West Woodburn on 8th March 1981. Having had a very busy day accounting for five foxes, hounds found again at 4.35 pm in Hareshaw Linn, running this dene for five minutes. The fox left the dene and made for Rawfoot Farm but was headed on the road and turned north for Hareshaw. Bearing right he came over the craggy ground of Callerhues. He crossed the Bellingham-Woodburn Road and ran down to the River Rede. Running up river to the village of West Woodburn, he crossed the A68 twice. He made for Corsenside Beacon, crossing the Otterburn-Bellingham Road onto Great Moor Fell with the pace increasing greatly. This stout fox again crossed the A68 onto Old Town Farm then on to Brownchesters and into Otterburn village doing a tour of the Percy Arms gardens. At this stage he was about a quarter of a mile in front of the hounds. The fox left Otterburn running down the River Rede on to Heatherwick and then Monkridge, where hounds caught him.

The only check that occurred was at the Percy Arms. This is one of the fastest hunts we can ever remember starting at 4.35 pm and finishing at 5.50 pm. The hounds ran 21 miles with an 11 mile point. No horses were left at the finish only car followers. Luckily the kennels were only a short walk home. I had abandoned my horse at West Woodburn and followed in the car. A truly memorable day.

Michael Hedley, *Great Days* (1997)

THE FOX

❖

THE FOX, MOST PERFECT ANIMAL

❖

I f an artist was desired to paint the most perfect animal in the shape of a quadruped, it would be not *a* fox but *the* fox; for they are all so nearly alike in point of symmetry; and, on examination, it will be found that no animal has so much muscle in proportion to its size, and the bone, like that of a thoroughbred horse, is like ivory; in point of strength of loins, nothing can exceed it.

Thomas Smith MFH, *Extracts from the Diary of a Huntsman* (1838)

The fox is called Charlie by hunting people, a sign of hunting's long traditions: the nickname was first used by foxhunters denigrating Charles James Fox the eighteenth century Whig politician. (Photo: Jim Meads)

MOST CUNNING

❖

Most cunning among all the beasts of the field is the Fox. Warlike of heart and wise, she dwells in remotest lair, with seven-gated openings to her house and tunnelled earths far from one another, lest hunters should ambush her doors and lead her captive with snares. Terrible is she to fight with her teeth against stronger wild beasts. The Fox is not to be captured by ambush nor by noose nor by net. For she is clever in her cunning at perceiving them; clever too, at severing a rope and loosing knots and by subtle craft excaping from death. But the thronging hounds take her; yet even them for all their strength do not overcome her without bloodshed.

Appian, *Cynegetica* (3rd century AD)

You're Vermin

You're vermin to a vast of folk
But glory to a few.

Will H. Ogilvie

"….the fox is hunted by the hounds only by scent, and very, very seldom by sight…his scent is weak and easily masked….he sets the course and the pace…", D.W. E. Brock MFH. (Photo: Jim Meads)

GREAT CAUTION NEEDED

❖

Great caution is necessary when a fox runs into a village; if he be halloed there, get forward as fast as you can. Foxes, when tired, will lie down anywhere, and are often lost by it. A wide cast is not the best to recover a tired fox with tired hounds; they should hunt him out, inch by inch, though they are ever so long about; for the reason I have just given: – *that he will lie down anywhere*.

Peter Beckford, *Thoughts on Hunting* (1781)

Vixen. (Photo: John Minoprio)

FOX HUNTING

— ❖ —

There are not many greater thrills in foxhunting than to be standing on the brow of a hill watching the hounds drawing a covert just below, and to see a fox stealing away from the lower side, heading straight for the best of the vale.

The visiting dog fox goes straight away across the middle of each field, straight across roads, rivers or railways, disregarding the coverts and passing over unstopped earths. Hounds really can run on with such a fox and they do run. To get a good start with a fox in early February and to notice after a half a dozen fields that he is a traveller gives perhaps the greatest thrill in the whole of the Chase. Those who can catch such foxes are the makers of foxhunting history.

Foxes will breed anywhere. They need no encouragement and only ask to be left alone . . . The only reason that a covert owner regularly fails to have litters on his land is that he does not want them, or that his keeper does not want them . . . For though big landowners may give orders, it is the keepers, the farmers, the bailiffs and the labourers by whom the foxes are preserved or destroyed.

The fox is an artist in his use of dead ground and of fortuitous cover. Think of the number of times you have seen hounds find a fox on a bare fallow, or in some rough grass. They course him to the first fence, and surge across the next field; a pause; heads up; no fox; round they swing (if they are a good pack); hit off his line where he has turned sharply under the same fence; run down a deep furrow, through a patch of roots, into a belt of firs – and by that time the fox has had a good enough start to go wherever he pleases.

After that he may run across the open for a while. That is your opportunity to cultivate your 'eye for a fox'. Do not look too far ahead, but watch the fences, forward and down wind.

Michael Berry, *Foxhunting, The Times* (1933)

HUNTED HE MUST BE

❖

Hunted he must be: if he is to exist at all in England it is his *raison d'etre*, and if consulted on the subject he would probably not wish it otherwise. He thoroughly understands the sport in all its branches. Pursuit by a terrier is looked upon as a friendly game of romps; a merry-go-round with a pack of harriers (not too big) is regarded in much the same light, and it is only the pack of advertised foxhounds (he is particular on the score of advertisement) whom he considers really worthy of the steel of his cunning and staunchness.

8th Duke of Beaufort, *Hunting* (Badminton Library) (1885)

Mr Sponge crossing a wet, deep country – John Leech illustration from Mr Sponge's Sporting Tour.

YOUNG REYNARD

❖

Gracefullest leaper, the dappled fox-cub,
    Curves over brambles with berries and buds,
Light as a bubble that flies from the tub,
    Whisked by the laundry-wife out of her suds.
Wavy he comes, woolly, all at his ease,
    Elegant, fashioned to foot with the deuce;
Nature's own prince of the dance; then he sees
    Me, and retires as if making excuse.
Never closed minuet courtlier! Soon
    Cub-hunting troops were abroad, and yelp
Told of sure scent! ere the stroke upon noon
    Reynard the younger lay far beyond help.
Wild, my poor friend, has the fate to be chased.
    Civil will conquer: were't other 'twere worse,
Fair, by the flushed early morning embraced,
    Haply you live a day longer in verse.

George Meredith (1828–1909)

THE MIDLAND FOXES

--- ❖ ---

. . . The whole population of the Midland foxes could be wiped out in a very short time if serious measures were taken, but in exchange for the pleasure man found in horse-craft and hound-craft when hunting the fox, he had given him continued life and on the face of things this seemed a good bargain. A fox, in a well-supplied district, is seldom hunted more than twice in a season, and if, like Rufus, it can survive several runs, the chances of its being caught become more and more remote. Hunting with hounds is cruel, however, and man knows it to be cruel; the whole of Life is cruel, or, shall we say, unfeeling.

Every hunting-man likes the chase because it involves some risk, and a man who rides straight must possess a good courage. So it is no coward's game. If, as we learn on good authority, a man's life is worth many sparrows, we may take it it is worth many foxes, too, and if we total up the number of fatalities in the hunting-field since the sport first began in England, we may think the fox wins (as he usually does) in the end . . .

'B.B.', *Wild Lone: The Life of a Pytchley Fox* (1938)

THE PRINCIPLES OF WAR

❖

. . . The fox is not human, the fox-hunter is not animal: it is impossible to compare even the physical, let alone the mental, reactions of the two. The fox-hunter would be disgusted with the life of the fox: the fox would be bored, with the life of the fox-hunter. So may other species of the human kind be disgusted at the thought of the fox's death, just as the fox would be bored at the thought of their idle, artificial, life.

Every man and every animal – as we can see by observation – fears death. But the brave man, and all animals, do not fear it until they know that it is imminent; it is the coward among men who fears death when the odds against, death are long. Watch a dog that has crossed the road and has been nearly run over in the process: is he nerve-stricken? No – he at once snorts about his confrere who was the object of his excursion. But watch a man who has been as nearly run over, or a woman!

The fox *must* fear death, but only when he knows he is going to die. So do the bullock, the sheep, the chicken, probably the sole and the cod and the trout, fear death, when they know they are to die. But the bullock does not tremble with the fear of death on his way to the slaughterhouse, for he does not know that death is imminent.

Why should the fox fear death throughout all the stages of a hunt? Because he knows that death is imminent? Nonsense! it is not: take the hunting reports in the daily press for a month, and it will be seen that, even among the packs whose sport is reported, one fox dies for every six that are hunted: yet those packs, hunting in open rideable countries, kill the greater proportion of foxes. Besides, there are innumerable cases, innumerable authentic cases, of foxes stopping to snatch up a chicken or a duck, with the hounds in earshot of them after a good hunt.

I have myself seen a hunted fox stop, with the pack in earshot, and take a duck from the side of a village pond, kill it, and leave it. I have heard of a fox in Northumberland, which was seen by several people – not all of them fox-hunters – to kill a chicken and bite off its head. He trotted on for a little distance and dropped the head. He stopped, trotted on again, stopped again. Hounds were within earshot now. Yet he turned back towards them and hunted about and finally picked up the head which he had dropped. Was he petrified with fear at the thought of his coming death? (Actually, he was not killed, though the fox which I saw take the duck, was killed within ten minutes.) Was he even mildly afraid? It is impossible to believe that he was.

And yet, it is hard to believe that he could not have been, for we should, had we been in his shoes, have been trembling with fear. The truth is, first that the fox is himself a hunter; second, that he is a wild animal, devoid of imagination; and third, that he is accustomed to every man's hand, every dog's jaw, being against him. Countless times has he been chased by the village

The Ledbury Hunt. (Photo: Jim Meads)

curs, by the sheep-dogs, by terriers, and has escaped – bark and yap their loudest though they may. Why should he be afraid this time?

When he knows that he is to die, when the pack is within snapping distance of him, then of course he is afraid. But no fox, no animal, no man, is immortal. Death comes sooner or later; and death is always fearful.

The fox-hunter may well find that his antagonist considers that the odds against the fox are enormous, despite the proof that only one fox in six – at the worst – is killed. Let him explain then, that the fox is hunted by the hounds only, by *scent*, and very, very seldom by sight. That his scent is weak and easily masked. That he sets the course and the pace; and that he alone knows the course he is to set, and that that course is the one which, of all others, he considers most favourable to himself, least favourable to the hounds; and that the presence of the hundreds of men, women, and horses, of which the fox-hunter's antagonist may make much ado, is a great hindrance, and no sort of help, to the pack.

What of physical pain, physical cruelty? Is it not cruel to chase an animal till he drops with exhaustion? Is it not cruel to tear him alive, piece from piece?

Yes, is the answer to each question. But the fox is not chased till he drops from exhaustion. He is chased until the superior speed and stamina of the hounds enable them to overtake him; besides, a fox, unlike a town-working anti-fox-hunter, is fit and hard, and he is accustomed to travelling each night, after his food and his love, as far and as fast as he has to travel five times out of six to escape the pack. Outside pictures, how seldom does one see a hunted fox gallop for any length of time? Yet a hunt*ing* fox quite frequently covers long distances at a sort of loping canter.

Nor is he torn, while alive, limb from limb. He has very sharp teeth, and knows how to use them. The leading hound has also learnt by experience that the only way to avoid a nip from those teeth is to seize, the fox across the back and crunch: instantly there is a broken back, and numbness. One more crunch and the fox is dead. The opponent will not believe this; let the fox-hunter invite him to travel to the Lakeland country and there inspect the body of any fox which has been killed by hounds (for, there, hounds seldom 'break up their fox' after killing him); he will find the corpse, though killed by hounds, probably devoid of any visible injury.

D.W.E. Brock MFH, *The Foxhunter's Weekend Book*

LOST OR KILLED

❖

'There is a vast difference in the meaning of these two words to us,' said an old Midland fox one moonlight night to his companions, 'and there is a vast difference in them both to hounds and huntsman. And although these two words stand as opposite to each other as do the poles, yet, which of them it is to be so often depends on a seemingly slight incident.

'Occasionally at the end of a run a fox is killed which is not the hunted one. Taking myself for example, I have on several occasions been reported "killed". Once I was so weary that I could not have stood up another ten minutes, but fortunately I disturbed a lame fox which hounds promptly despatched. Everyone believed it to be me! But both Jack and Tom knew better.

'I have had lucky escapes, due to various causes. Unlike hounds, I like to see a large and hard-riding field out, and a mob of horsemen at one end of the road, and a tumult of riders, at the other, boxing up hounds and huntsman. Jack so loves his hounds that his only thought on such occasions is to avoid getting any of his darlings kicked. This delays matters and valuable moments are thus wasted, while all the time I keep toddling along.

'When they do recover my line again, unless there is a holding scent, hounds can never run at the cracking pace at which they took me down to that road. After every check and delay scent gets weaker, so you can work out by rule of thumb that after a number of these halts scent probably vanishes altogether and the fox is "LOST" – the huntsman and hounds coming in for the blame.

'Some "know-alls" may say that a good pack of hounds will not mind being over-ridden, but believe me the higher mettled the hounds the greater the harm that is done. Occasionally by their noise and stench the hunting motorists will be the means of a bad running fox escaping, while on the other hand they will often so head a good specimen of our race that he dies like an August cub, turned back into the jaws of the pack. Had he not been headed this good fox would probably have run his pursuers out of scent or else honourably yielded his brush after providing a good run.

'A relation of mine owed his death to the chattering of a jay! He had stolen away, exhausted, yet unseen, and had lain down in a thorn brake. The huntsman had drawn his hounds out of covert and was making for home, having "lost" his fox; but on hearing the bird's cry he took his hounds back and dropped straight on to my unfortunate cousin's refuge.

'The condition of the pack plays an important role in classifyng us among the "KILLED" instead of the "LOST". I do not fear the best pack of hounds ever bred if unfit, while on the other hand a second-rate lot, properly conditioned, can fill me with dread. I have been hunted by different packs, and it strikes me that they all run very similarly at the outset, but the question is how they behave later on. Some seem to press you all the time, hunting more and more fiercely, while others on a similar scent (and you know, I am a judge of scenting conditions) seem to flag and lose all perseverance.

'Men, naturally, are only able to judge scent by what the hounds tell them, so they will say, of course, that the one pack was favoured by a good scent throughout, whilst the other pack suffered from scent getting worse and worse.

'Odd hounds may develop great sagacity at some time in their career. Luckily for us they are in the minority, and will usually not develop it before their fourth or fifth season. Even then the folly of men will often save us, since a fashion for youth and pace will frequently cause a wise old hound to be drafted after the cub-hunting is done. These old workmen are a great menace to us, especially if they have a good voice and will rally on the rest of the pack and teach the puppies to hunt in the right style. They may not be swift, yet by hunting close and turning with their fox they keep up the chase instead of checking and requiring assistance of the huntsman. A huntsman's assistance, however skilfully given, takes up time. Should a wise old hound have been the means of preventing the pack from checking on but three occasions during an hour's hunting, if you allow an average of three minutes only to the huntsman to recover the line, a wise old Nestor may gain nine golden minutes for him, besides greatly reducing the chances of changing foxes.

'Another great danger to us is a cunning old second whipper-in, one more renowned for his venery than his gallantry. But in these days of rapid promotions the old sport is becoming a rara avis. A small mercy for which we foxes are truly thankful.'

Isaac (Ikey) Bell MFH, *Foxiana* (1929)

'The Mockers', c. 1925, by Lionel Edwards, the doyen of twentieth century British sporting artists. An evocative work in gouache showing rooks mobbing a fox in a superb hunting landscape. [By permission of Kenneth Edwards]

THE FOX MEDITATES

When Samson set my brush a' fire,
    To spoil the Timnites' barley,
I made my point for Leicestershire,
    And left Philistia early.
Through Gath and Rankesborough Gorse, I fled,
    And took the Coplow Road, sir!
And was a Gentleman in Red
    When all the Quorn wore woad, sir!

When Rome lay massed on Hadrian's Wall,
    And nothing much was doing,
Her bored Centurions heard my call
    O' nights when I went wooing.
They raised a pack – they ran it well
    (For I was there to run 'em)
From Aesica to Carter Fell,
    And down North Tyne to Hunnum.

When William landed, hot for blood,
    And Harold's hosts were smitten,
I lay at earth in Battle Wood
    While Domesday Book was written.
Whatever harm he did to man,
    I owe him pure affection,
For in his righteous reign began
    The first of Game protection.

When Charles, my namesake, lost his mask,
    And Oliver dropped his'n,
I set those Northern Squires a task,
    To keep 'em out of prison.
In boots as big as milking-pails,
    With holsters on the pommel,
They chevied me across the Dales
    Instead of fighting Cromwell.

When thrifty Walpole took the helm,
    And hedging came in fashion,
The March of Progress gave my realm
    Enclosure and Plantation.
'Twas then, to soothe their discontent,
    I showed each pounded Master,
However fast the Commons went,
    I went a little faster!

When Pigg and Jorrocks held the stage,
    And Steam had linked the Shires,
I broke the staid Victorian age
    To posts, and rails and wires.
Then fifty mile was none too far
    To go by train to cover,
Till some dam' sutler pupped a Car,
    And decent sport was over!

When men grew shy of hunting stag
    For fear the Law might try 'em,
The car put up an average bag
    Of twenty dead per diem.
Then every road was made a rink
    For Coroners to sit on;
And so began, in skid and stink,
    The real blood-sports of Britain!

Rudyard Kipling

SWEET CRY OF HOUNDS...

A GOOD FOXHOUND

— ❖ —

The properties of a good hound are soon told. He does his best to find a fox; throws his tongue when he is *sure* he has found him, and not before; gets away *quickly* with the scent so long as it is forward; *stops* and *turns quickly* when it is not forward; *drives* it to the end *without* dwelling on it, or *tieing*; is *true to the line* without being too eager to get to the head and guide the scent; *sticks to his fox* when he is sinking in a cover, let the cover be ever so strong, which proves his perseverance and stoutness; quite steady from riot in the field; not jealous in his work; good-tempered in the kennel, of a vigorous constitution, and sound from head to foot.

A friend of mine, speaking of the merits of hounds, has this curious though not unreasonable notion – 'It may appear paradoxical,' he says, 'but it is nevertheless true, that one proof of a hound's goodness is, that he is never remarkable during a run; and there are many good sportsmen who would prefer a hound of this nature to one that is oftener seen at head than the rest.

'Of course a hound that is not remarkable is never last, or where he should not be, but holds the line, and is what is called by some a good line-hunter, which is the criterion of all goodness; that is, if he *drives* a scent, too, without dwelling on it.'

Charles James Apperley ('Nimrod') (1842)

Anthony Adams, huntsman of the Heythrop, wearing that Hunt's green livery, as he shows a doghound in the championship at Peterborough Royal Foxhound Show. Tony Wright and Michael Rowson, Exmoor and South Shropshire huntsmen respectively, are competing. (Photo: Jim Meads, My Hunting World)

A WELL BRED HOUND

❖

In truth there is no country where a well bred Hound of the middle size with good neck and shoulders, will not hold his own with any other sort that has yet been bred besides being far more pleasing to the eye.

Let us try to describe him in a little more detail. He stands not less than twenty-three, and not more than twenty-four inches.

He has a lean head, rather conical than flat, with a delicately chiselled muzzle; dark, full, luminous eyes, denoting keenness and intelligence, close-lying ears; small and pointed. His long neck, with the line of the throat quite clean, is supported by sloping shoulders at the foremost point of which his forelegs are set or, with knees near to the ground, plumb straight whether viewed from the side or the front.

His feet are round without being fleshy, with the toes close together. His fore-ribs are deep, but not so widely sprung as to push his shoulders forward. The upward curve of the underline is not unduly pronounced, even when he has not been fed for twenty-four hours. His muscular back is flat and straight right up to the point where his feathery and delicately curved stern is set on.

The thighs are wide and muscular, supported by straight hocks near to the ground like his knees. His coat is smooth; glossy and so supple that you can pick up a handful of it and see it glide back into its place the moment it is released.

A hound built on these lines would be difficult to beat in any country.

Lord Willoughby de Broke, MFH, *Hunting the Fox* (1926)

Mr and Mrs Nigel Peel (right), Joint Masters of the North Cotswold, with their champion bitch Grapefruit at Peterborough Royal Foxhound Show, shown by kennel huntsman Charlie White, and attended by puppy walkers Mr and Mrs Charlie Warren. (Photo: Jim Meads, My Hunting World)

WELSH FOXHOUNDS

— ❖ —

It is commonly stated that the Welsh hound of Glamorganshire of earlier date than these references, originated from hounds brought to Margam Abbey by the French monks. Certain present-day French hounds are so like the light, coloured, rough-coated type of Welsh hound that there is small reason to doubt it. The correctness of the assumption is further borne out by the fact that a very strong 'throwback' is constantly cropping up in the Welsh packs, in the *very smooth coated* black and tan, dark red tan, and 'mousy' tan hounds we so often see.

Curiously, this 'throw-back' occurs even more frequently in the crosses with the English hound, a case actually happening a few years ago in Sir Edward Curre's white pack.

Such hounds are almost indistinguishable from the Kerry Beagle, which possibly has been bred continuously to the type.

It therefore seems reasonable to surmise that this 'St Hubert' type of French hound formed a part of the 'makeup' of the Welsh hound, the English hound, and, in still greater degree, the Kerry Beagle of today.

Doubtless, after the French introductions, the Pointer cross was used in Wales, as was probably done in England, judging from the appearance of many hounds depicted in old sporting pictures and prints.

The Welsh hound, according to tradition, and there is small reason to doubt it, was also given a fairly strong infusion of blood from the Scottish deerhound.

The colour, the coat, and the rather long and whiplike stern of many present-day Welsh hounds all point to this.

There is, then, in purest Welsh packs of the present day, a great variety of coat and colour.

There are white hounds with black or coloured markings and coats both very rough and very smooth. . .

. . . How, then, can the English hound man identify the Welsh hound? Possibly this is easier than would at first appear.

Certain points in conformation are distinctive and are *always* to be found in the purer bred Welsh hound.

All appear to have a sufficiently good shoulder to allow them to move forward both quickly and easily with nose low to ground.

All are somewhat light of bone, back at the knee, long below the knee, and inclined to a 'hare' foot (the latter by no means always a 'good' foot).

They are low at elbow, and the hock is particularly low to the ground, far more so, for example, than in the modern English hound.

The above may help a little, but the outstanding feature in the pure Welsh hound is his *head*.

Brecon and Talybont huntsman Ian Hawkins showing champion bitch Sonic at the Wales and Border Counties Hound show at Builth Wells. (Photo: Jim Meads, My Hunting World)

The head is long from the point of the nose to the eye, which is usually full, generous, and of a rich brown colour (occasionally a shade lighter than the English hound man cares for, but this is commoner in the crossbred).

The *shape of the skull* is the most marked feature of all.

This is definitely sloped downwards towards the sides from a central ridge, culminating in a peak at the poll, very much like that of the setter. The skull is not 'flat-topped' like that of the English hound, nor is it 'domed' like that of the French 'Vendee' hound or the bloodhound.

Another most distinctive feature is the ear, which is always set on very low, and is long, long enough even for the ears to meet round the nose (for Welsh hounds are never rounded).

There is no call for us to say much as regards working qualities. The Welsh hound has no peer in the matter of nose and tongue among the many sorts of hound which are used to hunt the fox.

He is a 'busy' animal, never tired of trying, and although, as in other breeds, there are good and bad individuals, there are pure Welsh hounds living today (contrary to the general idea) which are absolutely 'non-riot' and 'non-change' to fresh foxes.

The cry of a pack of pure Welsh hounds on a rich scent must be heard to be appreciated.

Captain J.D.D. Evans MFH, *Foxhunting* (Lonsdale Library)

Berkeley huntsman Chris Maiden, wearing his Hunt's famous yellow livery, with hounds before putting them in to draw a field of kale. Hounds know exactly what is to happen and await their huntsman's command. (Photo: Jim Meads, My Hunting World)

THE KERRY BEAGLES

. . . For two hundred years or more, this private pack has been handed down in the Ryan family, of Knocklong, in Limerick. Their progenitors are thought to have been brought originally from France, perhaps by returning 'soldiers of fortune'. Hunted by that famous sportsman, John F. Ryan, the Master of Scarteen, these hounds are still rated as harriers, although it is many years since they hunted the hare. Noted for nose, pace, and cry, they are nearly always black-and-tan without white, although occasionally one is seen similar in colour to red Virginia hounds; and they have been carefully bred for performance, fashion and fancy having been ignored. They have all the physical attributes essential to activity, pace, and stamina, with no superficial lumber to carry, closely-knit feet, natural-shaped pasterns, not so straight as to lack spring, good shoulders, backs, loins, and thighs. The one characteristic open to criticism is their tendency to light-coloured eyes.

Mr Ryan's country is one of the very best in Ireland, not only for hunting foxes but for breeding horses. Galtee More and Ard Patrick, winners of the Derby, respectively in 1897 and 1902 were foaled not two miles from Scarteen and almost at their paddock gate was formerly a covert made entirely of sticks which always yielded a fox.

J.B. Thomas MFH (USA), *Hounds and Hunting Through the Ages* (1928)

The Scarteen's Kerry Beagles in full cry. (Photo: Jim Meads)

HURRAH FOR THE HOUNDS OF THE MEYNELL

❖

These good hounds in chase to the best won't give place,
For of good ones they're surely the pick
When the scent is breast high, swift as pigeons they fly,
When 'tis cold to the line close they stick,
For they can both find, hunt and kill, and the man who denies it knows nil
If your mount is a hack, pray don't hunt with this pack,
Or get down you assuredly will . . .

Chorus:
   Then hurrah for the hounds of the Meynell
   The world cannot boast such a Kennel,
   And a man must ride straight, if he'd not be too late
   To see Reynard roll'd o'er by the Meynell.

'Tis the first of November, the opening day,
At Sudbury coppice they've met.
There's a scent in the cover the knowing ones say,
There's a fox for a fiver I'll bet.
For it's a Tally-ho! forrard away, his line is for Potter's I'll lay.
If you're game for a lark, there are pales in the park,
Take a good lot of jumping they say . . .

O'er the pastures beyond they are racing like mad
As though they were tied to his brush;
Though the fences are blind, the real good 'uns don't mind,
For a cropper they care not a rush.
'Twixt the best friends, 'tis war to the knife, each vows he'll be first in the strife,
And the man that is in it will swear that each minute
Was worth all the rest of his life . . .

Now the good 'uns sit down, for I'll wager a crown
There'll be some wet jackets ere long;
From the brook they don't shrink, though it's up to the brink,
And the current runs deucedly strong.
Shake him up, catch him, fast by the head, for never shall truly be said,
That a Derbyshire man, when he's leading the van,
Of the biggest place ere had a dread . . .

Yonder's Potter's so snug where we're sure of a jug
Of good beer, and good bread and good cheese;
Throw the reins on his neck, for you've time while we check
To enjoy these good things at your ease.
But it's Tally-ho! forrard away, a labourer's viewed him they say;
Ere you reach Hilton Gorse you'll know whether your horse
Can not only gallop but stay.

'Moy oyes, e's a winder,' the labourer said,
'And 'e's gone past 'ere ten minutes quoite.
'Is tag it were whoite and 'is coot it were red;
Yo'll non ketch Bow'd Reynolds tonight.
Moy oyes, but yo' canna joomp theere, 'tis seven foot 'oigh very near.
There's a ditch at t' fur soide most tremenjously woide,
A's joomped it, boy goy, joomped it clear!' . . .

Now the front rank grows small, for full many's the fall
That their numbers has thinned since the find;
Some have bellows to mend, many pray for the end,
For they're getting most sadly behind.
But the customers sit down and ride, determined whate'er may betide,
To be able to say of that glorious day,
I was there when the gallant fox died . . .

See yonder he goes, you can see by the crows
That they are circling and wheeling above him,
Though the moment is nigh when this good fox must die;
Though we all want to kill him we love him.
See the fox and the hounds in one field, but he'll fight to the death ere he yield.
Ah, hark to that yell, 'tis poor Reynard's death knell,
The fate of the rover is sealed . . .

Chorus:
    Then hurrah for the hounds of the Meynell
    The world cannot boast such a Kennel,
    And a man must ride straight, if he'd not be too late
    To see Reynard roll'd o'er by the Meynell.

                            Frederick Cotton (19th century)

THE KING OF THE KENNEL

❖

The Bitch from the Belvoir, the dog from the Quorn –
The pick of their litter our puppy was born;
And the day he was entered he flew to the horn,
But rating and whipcord he treated with scorn.
    Gently, Bachelor,
      Have a care, have a care.

So eager to find, and so gallant to draw,
Though a wilder in covert a huntsman ne'er saw,
'Twas a year and a half ere he'd listen to law,
And many's the leveret hung out of his maw.
    'Ware hare, Bachelor;
      'Ware hare, 'ware hare.

On the straightest of legs and the roundest of feet,
With ribs like a frigate his timbers to meet,
With a fashion and fling and a form so complete,
That to see him dance over the flags is a treat.
    Here, here, boy, Bachelor.
      Handsome and good.

But fashion and form without nose are in vain;
And in March or midwinter, storm, sunshine, and rain,
When the line has been foiled, or the sheep leave a stain,
His fox he accounts for again and again.
    Yooi! wind him, Bachelor,
      All through the wood.

He guides them in covert, he leads them in chase;
Though the young and the jealous try hard for his place,
'Tis Bachelor always is first in the race;
He beats them for nose and he beats them for pace.
    Hark forward to Bachelor,
      From daylight to dark.

When the fallows are dry, where manure had been thrown,
With a storm in the air, with the ground like a stone –
When we're all in a muddle, beat, baffled, and blown,
See, Bachelor has it. Bill, let him alone.
    Speak to it, Bachelor;
      Go hark to him, hark.

That time in December – the best of our fun –
Not a mile from the gorse, ere we'd hardly begun,
Heading straight to the river – I thought we were done;
But 'twas Bachelor's courage that made it a run.
    Yooi! over, Bachelor.
      Yooi! over, old man.

As fierce as a torrent, as full as a tank,
That a hound ever crossed it, his stars he may thank.
While I watched how poor Benedict struggled and sank,
There was Bachelor shaking his sides on the bank.
    Forward on, Bachelor.
      Catch ye who can.

From the find to the finish, the whole blessed day,
How he cut out the work, how he showed us the way.
When our fox doubled back where the fallow-deer lay,
How he stuck to the line and turned short with his prey.
    Yo-yooite! Bachelor!
      Right for a crown.

Though so handy to cast, and so patient to stoop,
When his bristles are up you may swear it's who-whoop.
For he'll dash at his fox like a hawk in her swoop,
And he carries the head, marching home to his soup.
    Sess, Sess, Bachelor.
      Lap and lie down.

G.J. Whyte Melville (1821–78)

WHY HUNTING OWES SO MUCH TO BADMINTON

❖

At this summer's Badminton Puppy Show in June, the Duke of Beaufort saw the result of 50 years' consecutive breeding of his own foxhounds, when the doghound entry was perhaps the best that this famous kennel has yet produced.

He inherited the title – and the kennel – from his father, the 9th Duke, in 1924, and ever since then has bred with infinite care the pack whose forerunners had been in the family for some 200 years. The hounds which came to him on the death of his father were big and strong, as was the fashion in the early century. They were largely by Belvoir sires.

As the Marquess of Worcester the Duke had had plenty of experience in hunting hounds, since from 1920 to 1924 his father had allowed him to hunt a pack of the smaller bitches, with which he showed phenomenal sport, assisted by amateur whippers-in who were his personal friends.

The pack consisted of 14–16 couple, and he can still recall some of those hounds of which he was particularly fond, amongst them Dorothy ('16), whose two sons became stallion hounds when he succeeded to the family pack.

After his accession to the Mastership he gradually set about breeding a lighter-framed, more active type of hound. His first entry, in 1925, was exclusively by home-bred sires; the next year saw the progeny of Berkeley Waggoner ('22), one of which Wagtail ('26) became a notable foxhound and brood bitch, producing two Peterborough Doghound Champions.

The year 1927 saw further produce of Berkeley Waggoner; 1928 proved to be a red-letter year in the annals of the Badminton Kennel. Through that wise and dedicated hound breeder, Mr 'Ikey' Bell, the Duke heard of a dog down in the West Country who was making a name for himself and who might well prove to be a useful outcross sire.

He lost no time in going to see the hound in question and he liked what he saw, with the result that the subsequently famous Tiverton Actor ('22) came to Badminton, being lent by the late Sir Ian Amory for the season 1928–1929.

His was the same male line – to Four Burrow Whipcord ('05) – as that of Berkeley Waggoner ('22), who had already proved his worth. He was a light-coated dog in an era when Belvoir Tan was predominant, and was perhaps the first light-coated sire to have been used at Badminton since the time of the blue-pied Leveller ('10).

He proved to be a remarkable foxhound, flying gates and even fences in his stride; moreover, he was a remarkable sire. His grandsons, Autocrat ('32) and Fencer ('32), were probably the first light-coloured hounds to win championships at Peterborough since Milton Rector ('07) in 1910.

'Rest for the Weary', 1974, by Michael Lyne, oil on canvas, said to be one of a series of paintings inspired by the art critic Stella Walker's call in 1967 for a more imaginative approach to sporting paintings.

Another notable year was 1932. Not only did the entry include the above mentioned Peterborough champions, it also included four litters by South and West Wilts Godfrey ('28), that outstanding stallion hound bred at the Carlow by the late Mrs Hall ('the Miss'us') and given unentered to Ikey Bell. Godfrey was an instant and outstanding success at Badminton.

What the F.K.S.B. of that year does not show was the acquisition by the Duke of a little blue badger-pied bitch, Petrel ('32), pure Brecon in blood, who was given to Master (as the Duke of Beaufort is universally known) by Ikey Bell in gratitude for judging the South and West Wilts entry at short notice.

Master was allowed to take his pick, and characteristically – for he is ever broad-minded where hounds are concerned – he chose Petrel, despite her Welsh ancestry and slightly broken coat. She appears in the Errata and Addenda of the 1934 studbook.

Since then her descendants have been 'as sands of the sea, which cannot be numbered,' and hers is one of the strongest female lines in the kennel today. Moreover, she bred a Peterborough champion in Pelican ('35) who united two precious lines of blood, those of Tiverton Actor and Petrel herself.

The Duke has never been afraid to experiment, and another such trial was made since the war, when he imported a bitch from the United States, Elkridge-Harford Daring ('57). She possessed a wonderful nose and voice, and her slight lack of constitution was atoned for when she was mated with the iron-hard Badminton doghounds. This line is still maintained and greatly valued.

After the 1939–1945 war a new male line was becoming popular, creeping in almost unnoticed at first by the use of South and West Wilts Phoenix ('28). It produced its first Peterborough champion – from the Meynell – in 1949. In the next three years the Duke of Beaufort's Remus and Rector ('47) (two litter brothers), and Ringbolt ('50) were made champions, and all came of this obscure line, that of Glog Nimrod ('04), a pure Welsh sire, used by Sir Edward Curre; the blood being handed down via Brecon Paragon ('23) to South and West Wilts.

Meynell Pageant ('35), bred by Sir Peter Farquhar during his last year at the Meynell, had brought this tailmale to Badminton. Pageant was lent to the Duke during the war and proved a fine foxhound with great nose and voice.

It was an immense stroke of fortune that his influence was experienced during the lean war years, and it has proved to be an enduring one. His was the tail-male of possibly the most renowned and influential sire ever to be bred at Badminton. I refer, of course, to the incomparable Palmer ('59), who founded a lasting dynasty, not only in his own kennel, but in others as well, for he was used in a total of 19 kennels.

His pedigree is filled with the finest blood of the F.K.S.B. and his mating to Woeful ('60) (the alliance of two Peterborough champions of the same year) produced four brood bitches and a stallion hound. This family might be said to be the backbone of the kennel today.

Four Burrow Pleader ('38) is another name which is to be found repeated again and again in present-day pedigrees at Badminton. He was the great-great-grandson of Tiverton Actor ('22) and his blood provided a happy nick.

Portman and Heythrop sires (bred by Sir Peter Farquhar and Captain Ronnie Wallace respectively) have contributed greatly to the success of more recent Badminton hounds, Portman Pedlar ('55) being especially noteworthy as the sire of Palmer ('59), whilst Portman Grossman ('52) and Heythrop Craftsman ('62) have both been of great importance. Carlow Striver ('63) and Tipperary Growler ('64) have exerted immense influence in the past decade.

Some of the Duke's best doghounds of the past 20-odd years have been Distaff ('52), Tetrarch ('52), Dreamer ('53), Woodcock ('55), Dragon ('56), Palmer ('59), Godfrey ('60), Badle and Bellman ('66), Gaffer and Grocer ('68).

He regards the following as having been the most beneficial 'outside' sires of his Mastership : Tiverton Actor ('22), South and West Wilts Godfrey ('28), Meynell Pageant ('35), Four Burrow Pleader ('38), Portman Pedlar ('55), Carlow Striver ('63), and Tipperary Growler ('64).

It is almost invidious to single out any of the famous Badminton bitches, but one cannot omit mention of Posy ('63), Palmer's memorable daughter; Peterborough champion and dam of champions, who hunted into her eighth season, still retaining her beautiful outlines at the age of nine. Her line is very strong in the present kennels, and last year's Peterborough Doghound Champion, Pontiff ('70), was bred by her, as well as Beadle ('66), the 1968 winner.

Since he started to breed his own hounds, the Duke has won no fewer than 20 doghound championships at Peterborough and 10 bitch championships; a very remarkable record in just 50 years.

The Duke's most recent experiment with sires from other kennels has been the use of College Valley Bellman ('70), who hunted with the Badminton doghounds with great success last season and has been mated with a number of bitches this year. The progeny of Crawley and Horsham Farley ('70) in the past two years have been extremely prominent at the puppy shows, whilst the first-season hounds have done well in the field.

By judicious breeding during the past half-century the Duke of Beaufort has materially changed the make and shape of his hounds, whilst retaining the stout constitutions for which they are renowned. They have always been bred for work, and fortunate is the pack which obtains hounds from this kennel.

A glance through the pages of the Foxhound Kennel Stud Book shows just how numerous are the packs which have benefitted from the Duke's proverbial generosity. With the infiltration of this blood into smaller kennels, far and wide, we are likely to experience more and more surprises at the major hound shows, when possibly small two-day a week packs will produce hounds, 100 per cent 'Badminton' in pedigree, to carry off a coveted silver cup to some comparatively obscure corner of England.

Daphne Moore, *Foxhunting Companion* (1978)

HANDLING HOUNDS
IN THE FIELD

❖

I looked at my diary, in case it might amuse you, and discovered that I had hunted hounds on 3,895 days. I am very disappointed I did not reach the 4,000 but I had two very bad falls, and I could not go on another season.

I never hunted a pack of harriers or beagles. It is true that in earliest childhood I had two or three couple of beagles which I used to hunt whenever the holidays came along. I used to have meets in the Park and people would come along and say: 'Good morning, Master. Where are you going to draw today, Master?'

And from that rather poor joke to a young boy, my nickname became Master, which most people call me today.

I did whip-in to the Eton Beagles. It was the winter of 1916–17 when the war was at its worst, and I expect quite rightly the headmaster decided the beagles were not to be kept in being.

I had hoped to hunt them the next season, but all of us had to join the Army, and since then I am afraid I took to hunting foxhounds, and only unintentionally, without my permission, have I hunted the hare since then.

These are the qualifications which Peter Beckford in his great book wrote about the huntsman, and this is my text: *He should be young, strong, active, bold and enterprising, fond of the diversion and indefatigable in the pursuit of it.*

Well, those who have hunted hounds know there is nothing they enjoy more in life. They will leave their work, their business, their wife, their children, their home and everything else in order that they can carry on hunting hounds.

There is nothing like it, and I will argue this is true with anyone if they have once hunted hounds, and enjoyed doing it, whether or not they have been a great success. I don't know that I have been a great success, but I have just loved those more than 3,000 odd days I have told you about, although some of them were not very good ones.

Having thought it all over, one just longs for the next day.

Beckford went on to say the huntsman '*should be sensible and good tempered; he ought also to be sober*'.

Well, that seems an obvious remark, but there is quite a lot in it. Sensible is the most important of those qualities, better than good tempered; everyone can have a drink at times, and everyone gets angry at times.

He '*should be exact, civil and cleanly . . . his voice should be strong, and he should have an eye so quick as to perceive which of his hounds carries the scent; and should have so excellent an ear as always to distinguish the foremost hounds, when he does not see them*'.

The Warwickshire pack, watching and waiting, after marking a fox to ground during autumn hunting. (Photo: Jim Meads, My Hunting World)

I quite agree: a strong voice which carries a long way is of great use, and if you can see which hounds have changed the scent that is the way you will probably know whether you have changed the hare. There is no doubt there are hounds which won't change their quarry, and you must rely on them tremendously.

Now, here's an important point: '*He should be quiet, patient, and without conceit . . .*'

Everyone likes a good holloa, and nobody likes it better than myself, but too much noise is very bad indeed in handling hounds. The hounds have got to make the noise, and the quieter you can be the better, then you can leave the work to them without in any way putting them off, and the better they will hunt.

Beckford finishes up by saying: '*Such excellence constitues a good huntsman. He should not be too fond of display until necessity calls it forth. He should let his hounds alone when they can hunt, and he should have genius to assist them when they cannot.*'

The huntsman should certainly let them alone as much as he can. I don't know about genius in helping them, but a huntsman is either born to it, or he is not.

But even if you are not born to it, you can make a jolly good huntsman by carrying out all the advice that Beckford or some of the other distinguished writers have given us.

It is a true saying that a huntsman's fame rises and falls with the sport he shows; it's rather a gloomy thought when you are having a bad season.

Many men may not have the obvious qualifications, may not have a good voice, may not be good runners although they are beaglers, may not be very good horsemen although they seek to hunt foxhounds. Yet there are such men for whom hounds will do absolutely anything; they just worship them from the moment they first handle the pack.

There was a very famous man I am going to mention now who was wonderful with dogs, and equally wonderful with horses: the late Lord Lonsdale, the Yellow Earl, a great huntsman in his day with the Woodland Pytchley, a famous Master of the Cottesmore. He always used to walk about with about six dogs, and when he went into his room to have a meal, or to write, all the dogs knew exactly where they had to go and they went there, with just a nod from him.

He was my godfather and I used to stay at Lowther. He had a stallion there. The old stud groom could not handle it without walking into its box with a big stick, but I saw Lord Lonsdale walk into its box, pat it on the neck, and give it a bit of sugar, the stallion remaining as quiet as could be.

He was a very exceptional man who could really do things with animals, and not many of us are lucky enough to be like that.

I know that one does try to spend as much time as possible with hounds. It is not always easy and I am sure that many Masters cannot spare more than a few hours in a week to be with their hounds. I know it is important if you can be with them, but I don't think it is all that important. Of course, you have got to walk them out and get to know which is which; I would not deny that.

But I believe that when you have shown them sport, caught a hare or a fox, hounds know it and they will come to you perfectly well. As for feeding them, I think it is absolutely unnecessary; cupboard love and hunting love are very different things in hounds and in people.

The Quorn hounds in action in High Leicestershire: racing down a hedgerow with great drive and cry in pursuit of a fox only a minute in front. (Photo: Jim Meads, My Hunting World)

Hounds will go to their feeder when you come back from hunting, and have their meal, but otherwise having once been with their huntsman they will never look to anyone else. How lovely it is to see a Master having perhaps come a long way to a meet, and to see hounds looking for him, recognising his horse, greeting him, and showing their pleasure at seeing him.

My hero in hunting was my father, who was a great deal older than me and a very big man, who hunted hounds for many years – the same number as I hunted them, oddly enough. He was wonderful with hounds. I really appreciated the way he hunted the hounds; he had a wonderful horn, and a wonderful voice. He had hounds which he could absolutely trust not to change, not like we have nowadays. I think they had much better scenting conditions in those days.

My father did not ride hard in latter years, as he was old and heavy. Hounds would check and he would come up and ask the whipper-in where they had hit the line last. The whipper-in would tell him, and straight away my father would pick them up, and he would not go round to the right and round to the left like I do – round in a circle – no, my father would take them straight on and hit the line of the fox.

There were a lot of foxes in those days, and if it was not the line of the hunted fox, his old hounds would tell him straight away. They would stop and look back at him, and he would stop the pack, then hold them on a bit farther, and go away on the hunted fox – and they would probably catch him.

It is a great thing if you can really trust your hounds in that way, but I think to achieve this takes years of breeding them and practice in hunting them. If you do attain it, it is worth anything.

In my kennel there are two great lines which produce road-hunting hounds. One was by a dog called Worcestershire Weaver, which was bred by old Mr Arthur Jones who was a Master many years ago. Yet still those lines continue, and hounds in the pack which were especially good hunting on roads all trace back to Worcestershire Weaver.

Today, sadly as far as my country is concerned, not counting the M4 which has ruined a great deal of it, so many of the other roads are now so covered in traffic that you dare not let your hounds run along the roads in case some car comes round the corner at 60 miles an hour. So we have lost the means nowadays of really finding out which of our hounds are the best road hunters.

Whenever hunting hounds, I used to try to draw up wind, especially in big woods. Foxes tend to run down the wind a lot more than hares, although you may not agree with me on that.

Nearly always, great hunts that I have taken part in have started slightly up wind, until the fox has found that he is going up wind and they are getting close to him, and he has turned down wind.

With a hare I think you are more confined within what I believe is called 'the magic ring' of where a hare will run. Therefore, when drawing with harriers or beagles I don't think it is anywhere near as necessary as it is with foxhounds to draw up wind.

But there is no doubt that if you can get a hare or a fox to run upwind the hounds will probably run very much faster than they would if they ran down the wind.

I hope some of you read *Handley Cross*, in which Mr Jorrocks says that 'none but a huntsman knows a huntsman's cares'.

Well that's certainly true. No one, except a general commanding an army has more things to think about than a huntsman. There is nothing, in my opinion, more important than letting a huntsman alone. The huntsman should have as much freedom as possible.

As far as the pack is concerned, foxhounds especially must have drive, a word which is difficult to define accurately in hunting. Beagles and harriers are much closer hunting hounds, but the foxhound is famous for its drive, and I do not believe the foxhound without drive will ever catch its fox.

The fox keeps going on and on, and very seldom squats down anywhere, or stops in a hedgerow for you, unless he is really tired. To tire him, hounds must have drive to go with him.

Yet on the other hand it can be tremendously overdone. There is no greater nuisance than a hound that will drive on right through a couple of fields, taking all the other hounds with him, with the huntsman not knowing what is happening.

Last August I saw the College Valley hounds run into a great flock of sheep right in front of them. Hounds came to a check altogether, and they decided the fox had gone through the flock and got beyond these sheep. We were maybe a mile away on another hillside, and we watched hounds go on and hit the line again beautifully.

Directly they got the other side of where the sheep had turned, hounds threw their tongues and away they went like the devil. I don't call that 'wrong drive'; I think that was marvellous. Hounds first tried all round where they last had the line, and some instinct in them took them right on through these sheep.

10th Duke of Beaufort, *Foxhunting Companion* (1978)

Equally Good Hounds

❖

If one has two equally good hounds in every way, A and B, supposing A's pedigree is much better than B's is, one should most certainly breed from A in preference to B. But on the other hand, if one has two hounds X and Y, and X is beautifully bred but, perhaps, a bit slack or short of tongue, while Y is not too well bred but first class in his work, one should not hesitate to breed from Y in preference....

Many breeders have concentrated on some point or other of conformation, such as necks and shoulders, ribs or bone: however, I should advise against doing that, as, by so doing, one may lose general balance. Beyond selecting your type of hound and always breeding to it, I would not advise placing too much reliance on conformation. For, after all, one's hounds may have beautiful shoulders, fine backs and loins, good ribs and great bone, and yet if they lack the necessary nose, tongue and drive they will make but a poor show out hunting.

I would advise rather concentrating upon some working quality such as nose, tongue, stoutness or drive. Which of these is the most important is, of course, a matter of opinion. But personally I consider tongue to be the first and foremost quality to be aimed at. For however good a hound's nose may be, if he is short of tongue he will usually do more harm than good. Stoutness and drive are both essentials too, but without tongue, your stout, hard-driving pack of hounds will probably prove most unsatisfactory, for in the first place, they will be very hard to keep together, and, secondly, in many countries, they will prove difficult to follow. Having a really good cry makes much more for pace, in a pack of hounds, than is often realised. For one thing, hounds with plenty of music keep better together in covert and hence get away better together; moreover, as they usually carry a better head when running than hounds that are lacking in cry, they check less often, and when they do check, hit the line off sooner as there are so many more noses there to do so.

Besides all this, to me, at any rate, more than half the pleasure of hunting consists of listening to the cry of a really musical pack of hounds. I would advise, then, a new Master starting to breed hounds, to go for tongue, nose, drive and stoutness, in the order named, and when he has obtained what he considers perfection in these qualities, it will be time enough to start paying much attention to looks.

Sir John Buchanan-Jardine MFH, *Hounds of the World* (1937)

THEY WERE
A LOVELY PACK

❖

They were a lovely pack for looks;
Their forelegs drumsticked without crooks,
Straight, without over-tread or bend,
Muscled to gallop to the end,
With neat feet round as any cat's,
Great-chested, muscled in the slats,
Bright, clean, short-coated, broad in shoulder,
With stag-like eyes that seemed to smoulder.
The heads well-cocked, the clean necks strong,
Brows broad, ears close, the muzzles long,
And all like racers in the thighs;
Their noses exquisitely wise,
Their minds being memories of smells;
Their voices like a ring of bells;
Their sterns all spirit, cock and feather;
Their colours like the English weather,
Magpie and hare, and badger-pye,
Like minglings in a double dye,
Some smutty-nosed, some tan, none bald;
Their manners were to come when called,
Their flesh was sinew knit to bone,
Their courage like a banner blown.
Their joy to push him out of cover,
And hunt him till they rolled him over.
They were as game as Robert Dover.

John Masefield,
Reynard the Fox (1919)

THE CHARM OF HOUNDS

❖

It was 50 years ago that I first read that fascinating book by Sir Edward Grey, *The Charm of Birds*, and then last May on Exmoor I re-read the equally charming autobiography of John Buchan, later Lord Tweedsmuir and Governor-General of Canada and his words 'Fly-fishing became a necessity of life.' But is the obsessional charm of birds and fly-fishing really greater than the charm of hounds? I wonder.

The difficulty here is that there have been many more good writers on birds and fly-fishing than there have been on hounds, and it is easier to feel the charm of hounds than to analyse and explain it on paper. But does not the same apply to other great things in life such as music and poetry?

I think the reasons why so many men and women of intelligence and ability retain an interest in hounds and hunting not only for a number of years, but for the whole of their lives, are many.

First, a man or woman who is charmed by hounds is charmed by a living organism, whereas a fly-fisher who owes his interest to his Hardy flyrod, or a bird watcher to his telescope, owes his pleasure to a man-made instrument, which to many of us is something very different.

I realise, too, that an obsessional bee keeper lives and works with a living organism, but a pack of hounds who love and respect their huntsman reflect (and he sees they reflect) many virtues which are also considered human virtues, in a different way that I think a hive of bees does not!

As Sir John Jardine wrote, 'Breeding foxhounds, like breeding any other animal, is a fascinating pursuit. I know scarcely anything more interesting or, one might say, exciting.' But with so many animals you are breeding for material qualities such as milk yield, butter fat content, solids non-fat, wool, lean bacon etc. etc. But with hounds and racehorses you are breeding for something entirely different and, I think, infinitely more exciting. You are breeding for a combination of *beauty-cum-utility*.

The beauty, in fact, though useless on its own as is a show dog's triumph at Crufts, is an aid, almost an essential aid, to his utility.

No wonder it is so extremely difficult to breed a Derby winner or an 'immortal' foxhound. They have to perform and yet a good judge when he looks at them, will consider they are beautiful, because he can see from their conformation why they can perform so well.

Again, most hound lovers live in the country, and I think not only they, but also many who have to live in towns and 'escape' into the country, prefer it this way. But the country, of course, is more than 'the countryside with its woodlands and heaths, heather moors, downs and farmlands and all the wild-life of birds, mammals, insects and wild flowers that have their

Puckeridge kennels puppy show on a wet day. Kennel huntsman Tim Edwards shows hounds to judges Major John Berkeley in bowler hat, and Willie Poole in Panama hat and bow-tie. (Photo by Jim Meads)

home therein.' It is also the home of countrymen and women, who live and work and seek their recreation in it.

Many, many of us owe so much of our pleasure in life to such countrymen – in my case much of it to good keepers, because the majority of good keepers seem to me to be good and responsible naturalists as well. But what better introduction to the countryside could there be (and the politicians are always talking about 'access' to it these days) than following a popular, respected and well-run pack of hounds.

I do not see, moreover, how any man or woman can be a follower of any of our leading packs of hounds without being made aware of conservation and the charm of observing wildlife, or indeed forget the age-old and charming historical associations that hounds bring back. It is twelve hundred and sixty-one years since St Hubert died, yet still, in Dumfriesshire, Wales and beyond, there are hounds hunting who owe their colour to those hounds he bred!

As long as hounds hunt, there will be quarry preserved for them. I think one of the last true wild cats killed in England was killed in the Ludlow country about 1834 (the exact date is mentioned in Miss Pitt's autobiography), yet if the wild cat had been a sporting quarry as is the fox, we would probably still have him outside the Highlands, just as we shall always have red deer on Exmoor as long as we have the Devon and Somerset Staghounds.

Moreover, if it is the charm of hounds which keeps hunting going, it is hunting which helps to shape the beautiful kaleidoscopic pattern of our countryside. Here the aim has always been to avoid the vast arable acreages reminiscent of the corn prairies, but to break them up with carefully planted woodlands as fox coverts, well-kept hedges, field gates and bridges – acceptable to hunting people and non-hunting country lovers alike.

Much of Exmoor could, perhaps, be ploughed for barley, but where then would be the red deer and the enchanting herds of Exmoor ponies which now roam and are such a delight to those who walk there?

Hunting has been described, I think by the Chairman of the Masters of Foxhounds Association, as 'the golden thread running through the tapestry of our countryside'. I believe this is founded on the charm of hounds and I can think of no better description for it.

History, I think, shows us how easily ignorance can destroy and how hard it is for experience and knowledge to create, but I have no doubt that the greater the numbers of people who can experience the charm of hounds, the better for our countryside, our countrymen and our wildlife. All three at times seem threatened.

Sir Newton Rycroft MFH, *Rycroft on Hounds, Hunting and Country* (2001)

Huntsmen All

The Great
Mr Meynell,
'Father of Foxhunting'

❖

The great Mr Meynell was designated, by his admiring friends, as 'The King of Sportsmen' – 'The Hunting Jupiter.' He had earned those titles by the success of his practice – by the sport which he had shown; but, without an acre of land of his own in Leicestershire (the whole of his extensive estates being situated in remoter counties), he could not have carried on the war as a stranger, in the very heart of the best hunting country in the world, had not his conduct, from the commencement to the close of his career, been characterised by the deportment which distinguished a thoroughbred English gentleman.

He was, indeed, as much the *repandu* of the *élite* of Grosvenor Square – as much at home at St James's – as he was at Quorndon, or at Ashby pastures.

> The evil that men do lives after them,
> The good is oft interred with their bones –

but, with reference to this great professor of the science which he adorned, it has been universally allowed by all who knew him, that he was one of the most agreeable and accomplished of men, and that he was most justly estimable in all the relations of social life.

Mr Meynell considered horses merely as vehicles to the hounds – in which his heart and soul were centred – in the field; but he well knew the necessity of having beneath him the means of being with them upon all occasions; and even in those days, when three hundred guineas was considered as an ultra price for a hunter, he did not hesitate to possess himself of South, a little horse, barely exceeding fifteen hands in height.

There are different opinions as to his proficiency as an elegant horseman; but it is never disputed that his progress over a country was, like the whole course of his life, straightforward.

. . . .

He had a particularly clever hack mare, which he rode to covert, and which was ridden also by the late Marchioness of Salisbury This mare was the occasion of the invention of the spring-bar. The groom boy who rode her upon one occasion, having placed his feet in the stirrup-leathers and been kicked off was dragged by the leg and killed.

Debrew, Mr Meynell's valet and *maître d'hotel* (probably, as his name would indicate, butler also), a very ingenious and clever man, set his wits to work to prevent the recurrence of a like catastrophe. The present spring-bar was the fruit of his invention.

Mounted field of the Duke of Buccleuch's Hunt in Scotland, traversing a field to follow Hunt staff over a rail in a wall. (Photo by Amanda Lockhart, from The Art of the Chase, Adelphi 2005)

To him also was to be imputed the merit of a spring in a wooden leg, worn by Tom Jones, the second whipper-in.

This Tom Jones, if of less notoriety than his namesake, the hero of Fielding, was probably more distinguishable in the field. He was a capital horseman, and very active in the saddle.

The wooden leg, so far from being of any inconvenience to him, appeared rather useful than otherwise, in creeping by trees, gate-posts, etc., whenever they could contrive to keep this succedaneum nearest to the obstruction.

Jack Raven was huntsman; Skinner and Jones whipped in; and, subsequently, Joe Harrison.

Mr Meynell was somewhat particular in his diet, as everyone should be who cares for the preservation of those capabilities for bodily exercise.

–whose use
Depends so much upon the gastric juice.

He endeavoured to take the greatest amount of nourishment in the smallest possible compass. His usual hunting breakfast consisted of as much as a small tea-cup would contain of a pound of veal, condensed to that quantity.

His pocket was always fortified with a small bottle of stimulus, similar to that commonly carried in the present day; but, instead of eau-de-vie, curaçoa, or cherry-bounce, it contained a far better stomachic, in the shape of veritable tincture of rhubarb, to the use of which he was constantly addicted.

F. D. Delme Radcliffe, *The Noble Science of Foxhunting* (1839)

MEDITATIONS OF
MR BLOWHARD
(HUNTSMAN TO LORD FOXHOLME)

❖

I'm mounted the best, and everything liberal, with a Master who's all for sport. He understands hunting and he understands hounds, and I don't want a better to breed our pack ; but if he wants me to show the followers sport, he's got to leave a lot to me.

Yes, he knows all about hunting – as far as a gen'leman can; but of course he's not been through the mill as I have. I was second whipper-in to old Croaks for six seasons, when Jack Sprite was first. You understand what *that* meant. 'Sharp' was the word and no mistake. All 'fair hunting' you know, no 'patchouli' or 'rosewater,' *but sharp*, as I say. Good hunting, but as 'near the wind' as didn't hurt hounds, or disgrace our good name.

Croaks would grumble all the way home if we hadn't caught our fox. Whenever we found, if he passed either of us whippers-in it was, 'D— you, look alive ! Work your soul out till we catch 'im.' Ah ! And that's the spirit, too.

Croaks had a great command over his hounds. In some coverts he would let 'em spread out and draw as wide as you ever saw a pack draw; in others he would almost 'tuft' – keeping about thirteen couples or so at his heels all the while. It was a knack he had, and it wasn't very long before hounds learnt it from him, tufting or spreading out to draw, according to the sort of covert it was or its condition at the time of year. I saw 'em do it straight off for Jack Sprite the first day ever he hunted them, one time when Croaks got hurt. Shows how hounds learn things.

Croaks was the quickest to get away on his fox I ever saw. Odd times he would take 'em out of covert and swing them round to the holloa, cutting off p'raps half-a-mile – according to the wind. And I say, I never once saw him strike heel way. Other days he would hit the line right out, cheering them away. I asked him, one night coming home, when he happened to be particular pleased with me for helping him to kill his fox, 'why did you hunt the line out – instead of getting them out, like the time before, and getting a nick on your fox?'

'It was a different type of scent, lad,' he answered. 'It was a holding scent. And it would have upset them to no purpose if I'd interfered. The other time, though they did run harder in the open, scent was really of a more volatile sort. On a holding scent, d'you see, the length of a field or a minute lost (though I grudge both) is not so important as getting hounds well settled down to hunting their fox. But what we call a *volatile* scent is a quickly vanishing one. A holding scent gets only *gradually* weaker, like the taper on a good ash stick; but the volatile scent has a knack of going "snap" – like an elastic band.

'If the scent is of the quick-vanishing sort, how long to leave hounds alone is what you've got to decide. One minute behind your fox you can race him, but three minutes later hounds won't so much as be able to tell you he has ever been that way. The time when I let 'em hunt it out we were in the thin end of the covert; but the time I took 'em out the opposite end from the holloa there was all that thick stuff before us. Nice guy I'd have looked if they'd got on to another fox in covert and you holloaing the old customer away.

'Some folks,' he warned me, 'will tell you Croaks can get hounds to come to him even when they're *in full cry* on another fox. Don't you believe it, lad (and I wouldn't like my hounds to do it, either). But say nowt. What I *can* do is to time the right moment for getting their heads up. That moment may only last for a couple of seconds, but if the moment comes – I recognise it. I expect,' he went on, 'you'll be a huntsman yourself some day. Remember this : NEVER TRY TO DO WITH YOUR HOUNDS WHAT YOU ARE NOT CERTAIN YOU *CAN* DO. And with that,' he ended, 'I've told you the whole secret.'

With Croaks our orders were never to holloa if hounds were running hard in covert when another fox went away. We were to keep our eye on him as far as we could, and then to nip in and tell Croaks. He rarely made any answer. 'Does he look a good 'un ?' was the most he ever said. As to what he would do – that, as I came to see, all depended on the scent. I remember when, on a rare scenting day, we viewed a famous old fox away – an old fox with two white pads. Hounds were tied to another in covert, so I came up and told him about it. 'Stay with me, lad,' he said, 'and if they get out on a ride – or if the fox makes a turn and they check for a second – we'll have 'em out on the white-legged 'un.'

It was a full twelve minutes before that fox crossed the big ride, hounds in full cry. Quick as thought Croaks gallops straight on his line, foiling it towards the pack. One holloa, and he has the pack away, laying them on to our white-padded friend. As I say, there was a *holding scent*. Hounds struck it; but they knew it for a weaker one and a different one from that which they'd left. *Romulus*, *Remus* and *Clinker* all tried to drive back into covert, and I can well remember how old Croaks praised me for putting them on to the body at once. For with such a heavy tongue as that $1\frac{1}{2}$ couple had, they would have swung the whole pack to them.

Croaks's methods were always varying. During cubhunting he was, in general, very steady and quiet, and made hounds work every inch themselves. 'Learning them the game,' he called it, or sometimes, 'developing nose and brains.' But he would sometimes, suddenly, do something one didn't expect of him. 'just to sharpen 'em up,' he would explain to us whippers-in – after (as usually happened) he had killed his cub by that piece of unexpected interference.

Yes, I learnt a lot from Croaks.

Isaac Bell MFH, *Foxiana* (1929)

'One Draw More: The Quorn at Ashby Pastures' 1984, by Frederick J. Haycock, oil on canvas, depicting huntsman Michael Farrin with the Quorn hounds at a famous covert in the Friday country of High Leicestershire.

MEMORIES
OF RONNIE WALLACE

❖

There was no doubt that those three years at the Heythrop (1964–7) were wonderful. We had the best hunting in the world and, hunting five days a week, plenty of it. Bill Lander was the kindest man in the world. He did everything in his power to make life easier and more enjoyable for those who worked with him, yet commanded respect by doing everything correctly. Tom Bailey was one of the old school but always fair and understanding. If anyone suffered at Chipping Norton, it was the girl grooms.

Most of them had come straight from school, their first time being away from home. Mrs Brune fed them well, but they were classed as unskilled labour, so their wages were very poor. They had to pay for their own heating in the flat by putting money into a meter. Their hours were terribly long, particularly in the cubhunting season when they would have to be up hours before Bill and myself to get the horses ready.

They had chilblains on their hands so painful that they could barely hold the reins and were frequently being bucked off our well-fed horses. Yet many of them would come back for another season. The car followers were splendid people, coming from every walk of life, and always very helpful. They would often bring out special sandwiches and sweets for Bill and myself. We rarely went hungry, although I do remember one cubhunting morning in a field of turnips. I was so hungry that I had to pull one to eat.

A book has already been written about the Captain, but I am sure there is much more to be said. For me, there will never be another man like him. Certainly no man will ever match him in the hunting of the fox or in organising a country.

He has done more good for foxhunting than any other man alive or dead. All those who have worked for him hold him in the highest regard; his loyalty to those people in return is phenomenal. He was not an easy man to whip-in to. Only once did he praise me, and that was when I got to a very busy road just in time to save hounds being killed, although two minutes later he sent me home.

Fortunately, I was in good company, as he also despatched Mrs Fleming. Naturally, we both carried on hunting and when the Captain had killed his fox and was standing amongst his hounds, he turned to the field with a big smile on his face and said, 'I suppose Hugh and Mrs Fleming have gone home?' He knew I would not leave, as Bill was not out that day.

On two separate occasions I was pulled over the coals for stopping hounds. The first time, we were out towards Minster Lovell. Hounds had just got going and scent must have been first-rate, as they were flying. I was on the road when I saw them divide. The Captain and Bill

Sidney Bailey, Vale of White Horse veteran huntsman from 1966-2005, with the VWH hounds at Aldsworth, Gloucestershire, accompanied (right) visiting huntsman Michael Farrin. (Photo by to follow)

went with one half of the pack and I set off up the road and had the other half stopped as they turned to cross it.

Roger Dancer, a regular hunting farmer, rode up and congratulated me on stopping them so quickly on such a good scent. I hacked on up the road to try and get the hounds on to the Captain, when he suddenly appeared in front of me with the other half of the pack. He was raising hell because he had caught his fox and was coming to join up with the hounds I had stopped.

The second time was from Tom Bartlett's meet at Maugersbury. There was confusion from the very start with several foxes. Hounds settled to one and looked as if they were going away, when they divided. Again I set off, this time from high ground, and got the splinter group stopped.

I had not gone the length of a field when the Captain arrived, all guns blazing. His fox had gone to ground and it must have reached an earth he knew as he was boiling and he tore strips off me for stopping hounds. I just turned away in tears and set off into the vale, jumping everything before me. Mrs Wallace must have heard and seen what had happened as, after hunting, she made the Captain apologise to me, which in all fairness, he did.

He apologised twice to me in three years. The second time, we were hunting at Duns Tew. The Captain had his fox on its knees, but it was the sort of scent when hounds just could not get to their fox and he was doing everything he could to catch it. One minute it was in a fence with hounds all round it; the next minute it was two fences away. Bill and I were doing all we could to help hounds.

'Get on, you bastard, get on,' he yelled. I may be many things; but a bastard I am not. I think the fox was eventually caught, but by this stage I was not too bothered.

Hacking on to the next draw, I went up to Bill and asked him what he would do if the Captain called him a bastard – if he would question him. Bill said that of course he would. I said, 'Right,' and Bill said, 'Not now Hughgo, not now.'

I turned a deaf ear to him and rode up to the Captain. I told him that I had a father at home and if he ever called me a bastard again, I would go home, by which I meant Kent. The Captain thought for a second and told me that he was sure he had not called me so, but if he had, he apologised. He went on to remind me that hunt service was like the army; you have to accept whatever is said to you. That was the finish to that interlude in our lives.

It must also be remembered that, professional or amateur, the huntsman is always right. I love that rule; it is so true. One very good example of this happened during a day's hunting close to Little Rissington. It must have been a Saturday, as there was a huge field out. Hounds had been running well and, as usual, I had been trying to get on to see the hunted fox. I arrived just as hounds checked on a road, nobody with them. As I stood and watched, a small terrier appeared just as the Captain and the field arrived. The hounds took off up the road after the terrier and I rode up to the Captain to explain what was happening.

The answer was, 'Get it off the road, boy, get it off the road.' We all galloped up the road, rather like John Gilpin. Again I tried to explain to the Captain what hounds were hunting. He again told me to 'get on and get it off the road'. Having travelled the road so far, hounds turned off and marked at a garage door beside a very smart bungalow. The Captain immediately took away the hounds and hacked on to the next draw. On the way, he turned to me and said, 'Never, never let a fox run the road as you did today.' I think if this had been any other pack they would have caught the terrier amid much publicity. Diana, the goddess of hunting, was very much in love with the Captain.

A few weeks later he had good cause to be angry with me when we met at Upper Swell. Hounds found in a fence close to the meet. I was standing on the road when a fox came to me and turned to run up the road. I let it off, as I was sure it was not the hunted one. Well, if it wasn't then, it soon was. The Captain arrived and asked if I had seen anything. I told him a fox had just run up the road. But when he asked me where it had turned off, I had to say I did not know.

By this time, Bill had caught up with him and the rest of the field close behind, listening. 'I have told you before, never let a fox run the road. I'll shoot you, boy, I'll shoot you.' With that,

Captain Ronnie Wallace during his twenty-five years as Joint Master and huntsman of the Heythrop (1952-77). He provided remarkable sport enjoyed by large mounted fields in Gloucestershire and Oxfordshire, and achieved extraordinary success as a hound breeder. (Photo: Leslie Lane)

he took his hounds up the road and hit the line into Pole Covert. I slipped on and viewed the fox away. When we got back to the kennels, much to Tom Bailey's amusement, every time Bill saw me, he said, 'I'll shoot you, boy, I'll shoot you.'

In my last season, the Captain commissioned Tom Carr, a sporting artist from the north of England, to come down and do some work for him. Tom was very much an underrated artist, possibly because he did little work in the south of England or maybe because most of his work has remained in private hands. He was not only a brilliant artist but also a most charming person with a wonderful sense of humour, who sadly left this world far too early. The Captain had asked him to paint pictures of different incidents out hunting, not of the meet and hounds running. He did one lovely oil of Desmond Layne bolting a fox out of a barn full of straw bales, and the fox jumping over Mrs Wallace's head as she stood watching with the Captain. One day, Tom showed me his sketch book and two sketches of myself, one where I was jumping a gate and another of me falling over a wall. I was horrified and wanted to know if he had shown them to the Captain.

When he said he had, I asked him how he had reacted! 'He just asked me if that boy jumped a gate.'

It was not until many years later, after a Limerick puppy show, that the Captain commented on those sketches. Tom had very kindly given the Captain his sketch book before he died.

As there were nearly thirty horses at Chipping Norton, the hunt had its own resident farrier, who had a forge at the back of the stables. We often had horses brought in to be shot or horses that had died of natural causes to be fed to the hounds.

Many still had a good set of shoes on them, so Bill very kindly asked the farrier if he would buy any good sets from me. He agreed to two and sixpence a set. I soon had a few good sets and duly took them to the farrier, who paid me.

This went on for a while, until I became greedy. I had noticed where he kept these shoes and, when he had gone home, I slipped round the back, picked up two sets and put them in the valeting room. Two weeks later I sold them back to him. The fourth time I did this, I gave the farrier the shoes; he looked at me, walked into his forge without a word and closed the door. I had lost more than I gained, but I learned a valuable lesson.

Many people have said that the Captain should have gone into politics, and perhaps he should. But what would have been the gain for one side would certainly have been a huge loss to foxhunting. He never forgot anybody.

When my mother was working at the hospital, she nursed many of my friends before they went on to a better world. These included Tom Cooper, poor Guy Peate (who died far too young) and Mrs Vernon Williams. My mother has never forgotten how the Captain made a point of finding her when he went to visit Mrs Vernon Williams.

He is a man who will never be forgotten as long as foxhunting is talked about in this world. He is truly a legend in his own lifetime, and that legend will be there long after we have all left these Elysian fields.

Hugh Robards, *Foxhunting – a Life in Hunt Service* (2000)

FRANK FREEMAN:
ARTIST OF THE CHASE

❖

By the turn of the century the benefits of the industrialism once so spurned by the landed class were being enjoyed by all. The railway had meant that hounds and horses could go by train to distant meets; 'hunting specials' went from King's Cross to Melton and carried Oxford undergraduates to the Heythrop or the Warwickshire; the country-house party grew in size, and the train brought those rich, vital subscribers. The conditions of hunting had improved too. The land was better drained making it easier for galloping, and for the horse the clipping machine was a boon – hitherto, being ridden all day with a full coat was uncomfortable, being clipped with a cut-throat razor possibly worse.

Good fencing, drained fields and carefully nurtured coverts had made a hunting landscape that Hugo Meynell would have envied. His foxhound bred for speed was being hunted over perfect countryside and, with the improving techniques of hunting, there came legendary huntsmen.

The names Frank Gillard, Will Dale and George Carter were among those spoken of with awe, but the two names which dominated hunting talk before 1914 were Tom Firr and Frank Freeman. For when hunting people meet in conclave, wars, revolutions and depressions are set aside: what matters is the artistry of the chase.

It was said that Frank Freeman could speak to his hounds with his eyes. He had a melancholy, distant expression and spoke little. He had been born within the sound of the cry of hounds in Kildare, where his father was huntsman. Freeman made the progression that a would-be huntsman must make through the hunt servant grades: 2nd Whipper-in to the South-West Wilts, then the Tickham, the Brocklesby and the Belvoir, then 1st Whipper-in to the Belvoir and after that the West Cheshire. Finally he became huntsman to the Bedale and, two seasons later, at the age of thirty, huntsman to the Pytchley.

Hunt service is a vocation; no hunt servant would turn down the opportunity to hunt a leading pack, but the spaces are far between. Freeman's potential had first been noticed by Henry Chaplin – a legend himself as a Tory squire – while out with the Belvoir. Freeman was deputising as huntsman that day, and he had been blowing his horn too much. 'The Squire', as Chaplin was called, gave him advice. The day progressed better and, at the end of it, Chaplin recalled, 'He was so nice and modest-minded a fellow that he came half-a-mile out of his way to meet me.' Freeman thanked him. 'The ambition of my life is to be a huntsman. I am most anxious to learn,' he said.

The Master who had selected Frank Freeman to come from Yorkshire to the Pytchley was Lord Annaly. Their association as huntsman and Master was a model of its kind. Lord Annaly was an equerry and Lord-in-Waiting to the Prince of Wales, later King George V, and he had married the heiress of Holdenby House in Northamptonshire. In bearing and looks Annaly was the image of the aristocratic foxhunter and his presence alone was sufficient to command respect.

Unlike Lord Lonsdale he did not need to state his authority, it was already felt. His duty was to hold back a hard-riding Pytchley field and to give Frank Freeman the freedom to hunt his hounds without tiresome interference from himself or bother from the Pytchley fashionables.

The result of the Annaly–Freeman partnership was a decade of unsurpassed sport. Frank Freeman's dedication was such that he would never accept a lift back to the kennels after a tough day or in bad weather. 'I'd rather go home with my hounds; they wouldn't go home without me,' was his reply. And sometimes this would mean fifteen miles in an open horse-drawn van.

As the huntsman of a 'smart' pack showing an excellence of exciting runs and foxes killed, he became natural prey for flattery. A fashionable field – preferring the fast pace to learning about hounds at work – rarely grasped that the huntsman has a task.

It was well summed up for Freeman one day when a rich follower presented him with an ornate gold whip for which he had no use. 'I'd rather he get off and help sometimes. I believe he lost me the fox the other day. Them? They're no use to me; I never use them,' Freeman muttered.

A life in hunt service was understood by a good Master of Foxhounds, and understood too by those interested in the science of hunting and what lay behind the performance.

Apart from those who hunted to ride, there was a body of men who lived for the science, which, was dominated by hound breeding. The traditional English foxhound descended from those hounds bred by Meynell and his contemporaries, and in the blood line would be Mr Barry's 'Bluecap', Mr Gorbet's 'Trojan', and from the Brocklesby the famous 'Rallywood'.

There were the 'governing' kennels whose business it was to keep the strains pure and aimed at perfection – the Beaufort, the Fitzwilliam, the Belvoir, the Warwickshire and the Brocklesby. And in 1878 the Peterborough Hound Show had started, where prizes were awarded for the hound which attained the ideal.

A Kennel Stud Book was instituted and its compilation was carried out by the Reverend Cecil Legard. Legard was a hunting parson but he was better known for his knowledge of hounds than for his bravery in the chase. He had left his native Yorkshire to be vicar of Cottesbrooke in Northamptonshire and since Jane Austen had based *Mansfield Park* on Cottesbrooke, he found the Regency a more agreeable period than his own.

His dress was a frock coat, winged collar, tight-fitting trousers and a tall top hat. Legard wrote and spoke an antique English and his profound judgment of a hound could only be swayed by a different opinion from a peer.

Simon Blow, *Fields Elysian – A Portrait of Hunting Society* (1983)

'Sudden appearance of Mr Sponge at Farmer Springwheat's…Horror of Lord Scamperdale.' John Leech woodcut from Mr Sponge's Sporting Tour, illustrating the rascally Sponge gate-crashing a hunting breakfast where he was unwelcome to the Master.

ON THE 'ART' OF HUNTING HOUNDS

❖

I have been asked to write about the art of hunting a pack of foxhounds, which I have agreed to do with much trepidation, knowing only too well how little qualified I am to expound my views on such a profound subject.

There are so many different aspects of the Chase – so many different types of huntsmen and of hunting countries – which make it impossible, and indeed undesirable, for anyone to try to lay down any form of rules.

To start with, is the hunting of a pack of hounds an art or just an occupation? One certain thing is that huntsmen are born not made. Unless you have a natural flair for controlling a hound you will never make a successful huntsman.

There has to be a link, which I always term an 'invisible thread,' between a huntsman and his hounds, and the thicker and more unbreakable this is, the greater will be his success. Watching any great huntsman I get the impression that this 'thread' almost takes on the proportions of a rope – man and hounds seem tied to each other.

When one sees certain people who are totally incapable of controlling one small dog ('come here at once, Fido, and do as I tell you, you naughty dog,' and Fido takes not the slightest notice), or some shooting people whose dogs, if not anchored, will chase anything in sight, it is probably reasonable to label a man capable of handling 25 couple of hounds, by remote control, as an artist at his job.

But having been born lucky with the ability to handle hounds, further success will only be achieved through dedication, application, long hours and hard work; old fashioned virtues, maybe, but ones that have been our strength through the centuries and, alas, are so sadly lacking in some other walks of life today.

Huntsmen have always varied very considerably in their methods. At one extreme there is the huntsman who likes to try to hunt the fox himself, with a minimum amount of aid from his hounds. This type, for a variety of reasons, is a rarity these days, if not extinct.

At the other extreme is the man whose sole interest is to breed and train a pack of hounds to hunt and catch their quarry unaided, so far as possible, and only takes a hand himself as a last resort; if he has to do so more than very occasionally, he regards it as an admission of failure on his own part.

And then there is the question of what type of country he is hunting. In a grass country, with a large field of well-mounted followers, he has got to 'keep the tambourine a'rolling' to a certain extent, especially with short-running foxes or on a bad scenting day. If he does not satisfy the customers he will be out of a job.

Captain Ian Farquhar, Joint Master and amateur huntsman of the Duke of Beaufort's hounds, accompanied by his daughter Victoria. (Photo: John Minoprio from the Blue and the Buff)

In a less fashionable or a woodland or hill country, there will be less need, and less opportunity, to handle his hounds. But in any case the important thing is to leave them alone as much as possible – the more you help them, the more they will expect to be helped, and the less effort they will make to persevere on their own.

As a young officer cadet at Sandhurst, I well remember the great emphasis that was laid on the five principles of war as a basis for any military action; and I believe that these principles form an equally sound basis for the organization of a day's hunting.

First, OBJECT. To find foxes, hunt them in proper style, and account for them satisfactorily ; and, in so doing, to provide the maximum amount of enjoyment for one's followers.

Second, APPRECIATION OF THE SITUATION. This must take in every relevant factor: wind, weather, fox supply, shooting arrangements, farming interests, earthstopping, and many other things.

Third, RECONNAISSANCE. Some famous general was reputed to have said that time spent on reconnaissance was time never wasted. How right he was, and especially during cubhunting is this of vital importance. How stupid one looks if one arrives at a covert only to find there is an uncut field of corn adjoining it, or later in the season, drawing one's best covert blank, only to find out afterwards that all the foxes were in some kale two or three fields away that you did not know about.

One wants to find any new earths which have been opened up, gates that have become grown over and won't open, and in a big woodland, in which quarter the foxes are lying, what the rides are like, and so on.

Fourth, INFORMATION. As to the whereabouts of foxes from landlords, farmers, keepers, earthstoppers, roadmen, woodmen, and any other interested people. Only now is one in a position to make a PLAN, on the soundness of which the success, or otherwise, of a day's hunting depends.

When one comes to think about it, the huntsman's year is divided into three parts – summer exercise, cubhunting and the regular season.

During summer exercise hounds have to be got hard and fit but, equally important, the young hounds have to be taught discipline and good manners, and the older hounds given a refresher course on how to behave properly.

The huntsman's problem is to strike the right balance between keeping his hounds tightly bunched in – a whipper-in front and another behind – and giving them too much liberty. In the former case they will learn little or nothing and there will bound to be trouble later on when they find themselves unattended when hunting starts.

On the other hand if they are allowed to get into trouble – chasing a cat or a cur-dog – the damage may take a long time to repair (I mean damage to their good behaviour, not to the cat, although that may prove troublesome also!)

Much will depend on the weather – on a hot, sunny morning hounds will be much less on their toes and looking for mischief than on a wet, cold, or windy day.

The important thing is that the huntsman and his whipper-in must be always paying attention and anticipating. It is comparatively easy to stop trouble before it starts, but very difficult if one is a second or two too late.

The Prince of Wales hunting with Robin Gundry, Joint Master and huntsman of Sir Watkin Williams-Wynn's hounds on the Welsh Borders. (Photo: Jim Meads, My Hunting World)

Before cubhunting starts it is necessary that hounds should be stripped of any superfluous flesh. As well as being hard and fit, they need to be lean if they are going to catch foxes in thick, stuffy coverts, on hot mornings in August and September.

Some people, when they see a pack of hounds properly 'stripped out' for cubhunting, will shake their heads and say: 'If they look like this now, what are they going to be like by Christmas.'

In fact this is not applicable because, unlike horses, you can take flesh off a dog, or put it on again, within a few days.

We then come to cubhunting. To me, the first morning's cubhunting was always the most exciting day of the year and one hardly slept a wink the night before.

Leaving kennels in the half-light, the old hounds with their sterns going in a somewhat solemn and purposeful manner, their eyes gleaming with eagerness and delight, knowing that at last the boredom of summer was over and they were going hunting again. What a wonderful feeling it always was, and I am sure always will be.

I suppose the main objectives during cubhunting are the education of one's young hounds and young foxes, and ensurance that there is a proper balance in the fox supply throughout one's country for the coming season.

How, then, should one set about it.

The first thing that comes to mind is the question of 'holding up' in countries with small enough coverts to make this possible. Expediency must obviously dictate any decision over this to a very large extent, but I firmly believe that – all else being equal – it is a mistake to hold up tightly more than is necessary.

My reasons for thinking this are threefold. First, so far as young foxes are concerned, one's aim should surely be to encourage them to leave covert as quickly as they can, and learn that their best chance of survival lies through putting as great a distance as possible between themselves and the hounds.

These will be the foxes who provide good hunts later on. By rigid 'holding up' what will probably happen is that the weaker cubs and vixens will hide themselves, or creep into a small hole, whilst the stronger ones keep going until they are eventually caught.

I always like the story of the lady who was taken out cubhunting for the first time in her life and when asked if she had enjoyed it, replied: 'Yes I did, but I was terribly sorry for that poor man, Charlie, whom everyone would keep shouting at!'

Second, I cannot believe it can be good training for hounds, just as they are nicely settled on the line of a cub, to be continually stopped and turned back into covert accompanied, as it usually is, by much shouting and whip-cracking.

Up go their heads, their concentration is lost, and everything has to start all over again and very likely on a different fox. They can also learn bad habits. By racing round the outside of a small covert they often get a look at a fox, and perhaps catch him or, at any rate, 'nick in' in front, and thus become confirmed skirters.

Third, I believe it is important not just to hunt each covert, but also to stir up the local neighbourhood around each one. Foxes are generally bred in rabbit holes and hedgerows outside, and will probably use several of these during the summer months.

If one does not find these places during cubhunting, and make arrangements to have them stopped during regular hunting, foxes will tend to lie to ground in them – and good coverts, perhaps, will be drawn blank.

Ideally, I believe, one should 'hold up' for a short while until any old foxes and one or two determined cubs are out of the way (one does not want a five-mile point over a blind country in September) and then let hounds go away with whatever cub they are hunting.

If it is a big litter, one can return to the covert and repeat the operation. In such circumstances the use of whistles can be very helpful in order to convey information to the huntsman (who is probably inside the covert) as to what is happening outside it.

But, later on in the season, don't let whistles altogether take the place of the traditional method of signalling that a good fox has gone away. There is nothing that can replace a blood-curdling holloa, which sends tingles down the spine and gives at any rate temporary courage to the old or fainthearted.

Personally, I have always liked to do as much early cubhunting as possible in woodlands where hounds can concentrate on hunting without help or interference. Every fox killed fair and square under these conditions is worth ten easy ones.

It is during cubhunting, too, that the huntsman has to deal with the question of 'riot.' I do not believe it is a good thing to try to teach young hounds what 'game' (as opposed to domestic animals or park deer) that they may *not* hunt, until you have taught them what they *should* hunt.

Regarding hares it is comparatively easy and what I have always liked to do, on the way home after a good morning when they have killed a fox or two, is to wander about amongst hares on some friendly farmer's stubble fields.

If it has come out hot so much the better – I remember an old huntsman once telling me that the best second whipper-in one can possibly have is a good hot sun.

With deer it is more difficult as they live in woodlands in which the rides are not always as well kept as they used to be. Luckily hounds hunt a deer with quite a different 'cry' from when hunting a fox, which means that the huntsman can spot it at once and, with luck, can stop them with his voice and horn before they really get going.

In this case the horn should be blown with a long drawn-out discordant note which means 'stop doing whatever it is you are doing, and come back here.'

It also serves to warn his whipper-in and other intelligent helpers that he wants hounds stopped. A sensible huntsman will make as much use as possible of his old hounds to help him train his young entry, in the same way as shepherds do when teaching their puppies.

It always amused me to watch the technique of the older hounds when a young offender was rated back to the pack. With hackles up, they crowd round him growling and cursing, and I am sure that whatever it is that they say to him has much more effect than the ministrations of any whipper-in.

With all riot, if the old hounds are steady, there is no great problem; if they are not, there will be trouble all through the season and a lot of good hunts will be spoilt until such time as the trouble is rectified.

And so to the regular season, during which good sport will depend very largely on the success or otherwise of the huntsman's training of his hounds during the summer and autumn.

I think I had better steady up and just deal with a few specific points which will, or may, arise during a day's hunting.

First of all I think a huntsman should make every effort to unbox his hounds a few miles short of the meet. This gives them a chance to get the petrol fumes out of their noses, to 'tune in' to the prevailing scenting conditions of the day, and to empty themselves.

In most countries one has to use hound-vans these days owing to the dangerous traffic on the roads, but I am sure that hounds used to be much steadier, and make much more sense, in the days when we were able to hack on ten or twelve miles to the meet.

Next, how best should a huntsman attempt to 'draw' his coverts? As a general rule upwind and, particularly in large woodlands, it pays dividends to go out of his way if necessary in order to get the right way of the wind.

He should give his hounds plenty of time and encourage them to quest into the thick stuff, which they will only do if they are quite certain that he will not then move hurriedly on, or gallop off to a distant holloa, leaving them stranded in the middle of an impenetrable jungle of thorn or briar.

On the other hand, in small or bare coverts, it may sometimes be advisable to 'draw' down the wind, and, perhaps, touch your horn two or three times, so that the fox can get on his legs before hounds find him and so avoid getting 'chopped.'

On rare occasions when a well-known old dog-fox, who has provided good hunts in the past, is known to inhabit a thick covert in company with lesser colleagues, one may hold up one's hounds at the upwind end of the covert and stand there blowing one's horn for a few minutes.

The chances are that the good fox will leave in a hurry, whereupon you can slip your hounds quickly round the outside of the covert and get a flying start with him. There is nothing more maddening than to hear a good fox holloaed away and one cannot get one's hounds because they are running hard with a cub or vixen inside covert.

Incidentally, the wind plays a vastly more important role in hunting, and indeed in shooting and fishing too, than most people give it credit for. If a fox runs up the wind, then all is plain sailing and he will have to hurry in order to reach refuge in the earth for which he is probably making.

But, preferably, foxes run downwind, at any rate until they reach strange country and then they may start to circle towards their home.

But in a real gale of wind they will mostly run across it, which produces an interesting and puzzling situation for the huntsman until he cottons on to what is happening. In fact hounds are running perhaps 100 yards or more downwind of where the fox actually went because his scent is drifting rapidly with the wind.

If the fox, for one reason or another, veers up closer into the wind his scent suddenly fails to carry as far as the point at which hounds are running, with the result that they throw up, perhaps in the middle of a field, for apparently no reason, as if the fox has just disappeared into the ground or been wafted into the air by some friendly helicopter.

Captain Ronnie Wallace, near the finish of his career as one of the greatest huntsmen of the twentieth century, at the end of a day hunting the Exmoor hounds. He was Joint Master of the Exmoor from 1977 until his death in 2002, aged eighty-two. (Photo: Jim Meads, My Hunting World.)

All the huntsman has to do is to hold them up into the wind until they hit it off and go racing away again. Under these conditions, especially in very open country, I remember several occasions when this process has had to be continually repeated.

Let us revert, however, to the point when hounds have successfully drawn a covert and found perhaps more than one fox and are running in two or three lots. Obviously the huntsman wants to get his hounds away with the first fox that leaves because this is probably the fox who will provide the best hunt.

He should do everything possible to achieve this but must resist the temptation of going away with only half the pack, and hoping his whipper-in will be able to 'stop' and collect the remainder and bring them on.

The vital thing between huntsman and hounds is that each should trust each other implicitly and feel complete confidence that neither will play a fast ball on the other. More than anything else hounds hate to be deserted and left behind through no fault of their own and doghounds particularly resent such treatment and will cease to cooperate.

Even with a pack of hounds that is absolutely trustworthy it is sometimes difficult for a huntsman to retain faith in hounds against seemingly concrete evidence that they are wrong. Many is the time that I have been told by would-be helpful motorcar followers, or slightly more scornful mounted ones, that my hounds were hunting a hare, or more than one, which were evident for all to see.

In fact what has actually happened is that the fox had gone by before the informant arrived, and the hares were running the same line behind him. On these occasions some hounds may seem to be a bit hesitant but trust them and a few fields farther on, where the hare has turned aside, they will all drive on together again with renewed confidence and vigour.

Hounds hunting the line of a fox, particularly on a poor scent or at the end of a hunt when he is tiring and running short, requires an intense amount of concentration which, once broken, is very hard to recapture.

Thus it is of vital importance that the field should not press on them too closely and, if the huntsman has to help, he should do so very quietly and just 'nudge' them along. If he hurries them and gets their heads up, the fox will generally escape him.

Ninety-nine times out of 100, when hounds check and are left alone and given time, they will either hit it off for themselves, or, failing this, convey to the watching huntsman the direction in which they know their fox has gone.

Hounds definitely have a sort of sixth sense – fox sense I call it – and in certain hounds this is developed to a tremendous degree, which of course is worth untold gold to a discerning huntsman. I have been lucky enough to have had several such hounds during my lifetime but one in particular – Portman Pedlar ('55) – stands out by himself.

When hounds had tried and failed to recover the line, he would often leave the pack and literally 'push off' into the blue. All one had to do was to pick up the rest of the pack and follow him as quickly as one could because he didn't waste much time.

He would go for perhaps as much as half a mile or more before hitting off the line and telling one so in no uncertain way; he had a great voice.

Peter Jones, long-serving huntsman of the Pytchley (1971-2005) taking hounds across country after an opening meet when the country was still very green, with whipper-in Richard Emmott. (Photo: Jim Meads, My Hunting World)

One season I lent him to my friend the Duke of Beaufort and, on his very first day out, hounds checked on the runway of a disused aerodrome. After a minute or two, Major Gundry suddenly heard a hound hunting right on beyond the aerodrome, and, of course it was Pedlar; he subsequently sired the Duke's famous dog Palmer ('59).

Sir Peter Farquhar MFH, *Foxhunting Companion* (1978)

Time and How to
Use It

❖

Time and how to use it is the essence of hunting. It governs every stage in the day. The clock ticks on in the morning. How long will it take to dress properly without an ugly rush and perhaps a spur strap breaking at a critical moment? How long to get the car to the meet and park it? How long to manoeuvre the lorry into a position where it will not block road or gateway, or force riders to mount on somebody's nicely kept grass? I am a firm opponent of hounds and horses being unboxed at the meet – people tend to ride away with their tail bandages still on – and there is no case for haste when it can be avoided, nor should there ever be.

There is the question of the time at which hounds should meet. In early season hunting, this is relevant. Like most professional Hunt staff, I much prefer mornings to evenings. One can hunt early, return home in time to keep abreast of the day's agenda, and then prepare for hunting again next morning. We had an evening meet once with the Eton Beagles, and hounds had to be stopped in the dark. I said I would never do it again. Early is always better than late.

When hunting proper begins, the meet time must suit other people in addition to huntsman and staff. Some packs, the Exmoor being one, have followers from a distance staying at local hotels; they like a proper breakfast before coming out. Farmers may have milking to do, and setting fair afterwards. To allow for all this, we meet at eleven am in the regular season. In big countries, where many people have second horses, a good rule is to advertise the meet at 10.45, and to move off at eleven o'clock. This takes account of those people who are good enough to entertain the Hunt at their houses, and allows fifteen minutes for the social side to be enjoyed by hosts and guests alike.

When I was a boy, lawn meets were quite exceptional and special occasions. Happily nowadays they are very regular. Much depends on the whereabouts of the first draw. If this is a mile or so's hack away, hounds must get going and can settle en route. Otherwise a nice little corner nearby, where there is a possibility of a fox, is very handy for easing the time-pressure, and allowing the field to sort themselves out. Of course in a moorland country hounds can be drawing a second after they move off, and everybody knows this.

There is also the question of those people who lack time-awareness and arrive late. At the Heythrop, I had the idea of going back to wartime and meeting at ten o'clock. We tried it, but it was not altogether popular. In one discussion a charming lady follower who milked her own house cows put the issue with total realism, saying, 'I don't think it matters in the slightest what time you meet, as I come when I am ready.'

If people are persistently late, some Masters become annoyed and pull rank. Messages are sent out to culprits, via the secretary, and feathers are ruffled. I do not think this makes the slightest difference either. A better way is to alter the draw, so that nobody can be sure where hounds will be. Perhaps the huntsman is lucky enough to have a surprise draw up his sleeve, so that riders arriving at twenty past eleven find the hounds in full cry and quite a long way off. That is the most effective way of sharpening up the punctuality of some ladies and gentlemen. Those who arrive late, and cut across country to meet the hounds – and probably the fox – are an abomination.

It is with the time factor in mind that a Master plans his day. Blessed is the country where the meets are still given in the local papers, where earth-stopping is widely practised – and where the draw can be altered according to circumstances. Never is time more vital than at the draw.

It is very unsatisfactory when a huntsman goes into a thick place and rushes the drawing of it. That should be done thoroughly. However, there come moments later in the day, say two o'clock or so, when not much has gone on, when the huntsman must modify his plans. It is no good, not having had a hunt, to go on poking about unlikely places when he should really go to the certain find if he is lucky enough to have one handy. This brings us to the quandary between being in 'a bad hurry' and being too slow. We used to say that a bad professional is forever hurrying when he should be taking it steady, and a bad amateur is too slow to keep warm. The truth is that any huntsman must have a clock ticking in his head, rather like a race-rider.

This mental clock is particularly important when going into covert. When, say, hounds single out a fox from among several afoot, and the huntsman hears a holloa from a trusted voice in the direction he wants to go, he must know three things already – what sort of scenting terrain he is in, the conditions of the day, and whether he can get the hounds on to the line.

The clock ticks on, pressing him to assess instantly whether he can get hounds away in the next two minutes on the fox he would like to hunt, or if it is already too late. Much depends on whether he has seen the hunted fox, and if that fox looks like going somewhere, or whether it is a better bet to wait for another to go away. Also, if a huntsman wants a fox to face open country (particularly into the wind, which can be very important when hounds are settling to the line) there is a case for giving the fox a little bit of room, and not crowding him too early.

When I was hunting the Cotswold hounds – which is a fleeting scenting country – they usually needed to be on good terms with their foxes. One Christmas I went out with the Duke of Beaufort's near Chipping Sodbury, and the fox was holloaed away by Ted Reed. In my young way I was much impressed with the time taken by the Duke to get his hounds out of a wood. Right on time, the gate was open, Ted was there, and away they went. I asked the Duke about it later, and he told me he had known precisely how good a scenting country it was there, and so he knew how long he had in hand. That is timing, perfect timing.

Then there is the matter of time at the check. Hunting is a 'hoorooshing' sport and in most countries where you can ride, followers want to keep going with pace and no delay. In these days, because it is more difficult to get about the country, hounds may already have had their chance to 'do their thing'. Then it is time for the huntsman to do his. I do not support the idea of the chap who smokes two cigarettes while hounds are at fault. However, I have been impressed with Tony Wright, our Exmoor huntsman now. He gives the hounds more time than, perhaps, I would have done when I was his age. But he does not waste time. He and they recover the line in a nice way. There is a great difference between giving time and squandering it. As long as the hounds are doing something sensible, and the Hunt staff are also doing something sensible, all is well.

Most checks are imperceptible. But a huntsman is forever anticipating a difficulty. Perhaps it is resolved, perhaps it fails to materialise. Even so, only the very unwise are not constantly alert for trouble. That is why, on the whole, the best huntsmen are criticised for being austere. You cannot gallop along singing, 'It's a fine hunting day' and expect to be a great huntsman.

The distance, given in time, which the fox puts between himself and the hounds, is obviously of paramount importance. Years ago Ikey Bell demonstrated the quality of hounds' noses in the South and West Wilts country by taking them off the line (or they may have run to ground) of the fox they were hunting and, he knowing of another, putting hounds on it, twenty minutes or more behind this second pilot. By this he showed how his hounds could work out the line and hunt up to their fox. We can still do the same in some of our hill countries in the West, in Wales and in the North. If necessary, hounds can hit the line of a fox that has been gone for some time.

We had an interesting example on Exmoor recently. It was a very wild and difficult day, and we were hunting foxes that had not previously met hounds. Eventually a knowledgeable lady said she had seen a fox go a certain way, but some time before – ten minutes or so – which in those conditions was rather a long time. However these hounds, hunting downwind, soon settled. Two miles later I saw them still only trotting along. Then they got on terms and away they went again. The hunt did not succeed, but it was interesting to see how they had worked up to the fox.

In most countries nowadays, with all the modern difficulties, the aim is to get away on terms. That means probably within four or five minutes of the fox going away from the covert. But sometimes you go away 'right on his back', say out of a hedgerow or whatever. With those foxes, as long as they get to the first hedge, they will be all right. But a fox pressed too hard to start with may not give the run expected. When some distance has been put between himself and the pack, he will do his own thing. He has then no need to hurry. He knows all about time. For the hunt, however, progress is the thing.

An ideal run comes when the fox is quite a distance in front of the hounds. In the end, for a successful run, they must start closing that gap. A dashing twenty minutes is very exhilarating, a pretty quick forty minutes is very good for the hounds, and probably as much as a horse wants at high pressure until he has had a breather. A hunt of an hour to one hour and twenty minutes is also very good. Thereafter one is dealing with longer hunts of two hours and more, and their different demands.

When we had big fields out in Heythropia, I thought it ideal to have a hound hunt for the ladies and gentlemen of say one hour forty minutes or two hours in the morning, with the field master exerting his charms and his skills. In the afternoon, when many people had gone home,

'The Duke of Beaufort with his hounds in Badminton Park', 1973, by Madeleine Selfe. The 10th Duke, a great hound breeder, was Master of his family pack for sixty years (1924-84) and hunted them for forty-seven years. He was widely known as 'Master' and was leader of the foxhunting world for most of the twentieth century. This picture was given to the Duke by the Duchess to celebrate their golden wedding anniversary.

then (as Richard Fleming once described it) the huntsman 'throws away cap and gown', the pressure is on, and even when hounds check, they are soon gone again. That is the true thrill of the chase.

It is absolutely correct that a fox can either travel quickly, or far, but he cannot do both. He has a good turn of speed. He can really hustle. But one does not see a fox going like a lamplighter as soon as he is out of hounds' immediate orbit. If every fox, as depicted by ignorant critics, is just being pursued headlong from A to B, hounds would catch every one of them. But that is not the way of it. He takes advantage of his knowledge of the country, and of his skills over scent.

Captain Ronnie Wallace MFH, *Ronnie Wallace – A Manual of Foxhunting* (2003)

Mr Sponge in a bog – 'The impetuous Hercules rushed and reared onwards as if to clear the wide expanse; and alighting still lower, shot Sponge right overhead in the middle.' John Leech illustration from Mr Sponge's Sporting Tour.

The Fun of It ...

LUCY ON LEOTARD –
THE LADY WHIPPER-IN

❖

HABIT in the hunting-field was quite an unknown article in the Heavyside country, where nearly all the ladies had ample domestic duties to occupy them, and the gentlemen found it was about as much as they could manage to mount themselves, and, moreover, had no particular fancy for being outdone by their wives; so the first flaunting of Lucy's elegant fan-tailed, blue and black braided habit, as she rode along with Facey and the hounds, created quite a sensation, which was little allayed by seeing it was borne by the refractory Leotard. Not only was it borne by Leotard, but the fair equestrian was absolutely going to act the part of whipper-in to the hounds: Swig and Chowey having got such 'juices' of shakes as Chowey said, by their upset, as made them more like mummies than men. But for this untoward accident Facey might have passed Lucy off for a chance lady who had come down to look at the horse.

The meet was on Calderlaw Common – not a common by courtesy, as many now are, but a real unenclosed common of wildness and waste – rather a favourite fixture, for the roads were most accommodating, the country open, and, without being hilly, was undulating, very favourable for seeing, in fact; moreover, being mostly drained land, there were no agonising ditches to add to the terror of too formidable fences. So there was generally less 'which way, Tomkins?' – 'which way, Jenkins?' when the hounds met there, than when they were lower down in the vale.

The early birds of the hunt, those who rode their own horses on, Friar, Friskin, Coglin, and others, were now surprised by the unwonted appearance of a habit.

'What's up now?' exclaimed Friar.

'Woman, as I live!' rejoined Friskin.

'Why, it's Mrs. Rowley Rounding,' muttered Coglin, staring intently.

'Not a bit of it,' replied the first speaker, who knew her figure better.

'It's her horse, however,' observed Friskin, eyeing the cream-colour as he ambled along.

'Was,' rejoined Coglin, who knew all about the sale and return.

And now, as the widely-spreading pack came straggling along the green lane leading on to the common, there was a general move that way to see who it was.

'I'll tell you what, I shouldn't be 'sprised,' said Coglin, seizing Friar by the left arm, and whispering in his ear as they rode along together, 'I'll tell you what, confidentially, I shouldn't be 'sprised if it's that Mrs. What's-her-name from the "West-end Swell".'

'Not Mrs. Spicer

'The Muddy Gateway', 1985, by Michael Lyne. Note the bold rider jumping the fence cleanly while the others get splashed with mud in the gateway.

'Oh no, that's the landlady. This is the mysterious lady who has just come down. My groom heard of her yesterday.'

'Indeed!' exclaimed Friar, now staring intently, wondering what Mrs. Friar would say when she heard of it.

Facey, who gave his hounds plenty of liberty on the road, now rather contracted their freedom by a gentle rate to Favourite, who had got somewhat too far in advance, and the head receding, while the tail advanced, the pack came up in a perfect cluster of symmetrical beauty. There's a lot of charmers, thought Facey, as he looked them over, and then proceeded to nod to, and 'how are ye?' the field. Our master's greetings were responded to, but the parties evidently seemed as if they expected something more; viz., to be introduced to the lady. This, however, Facey had no notion of doing, keeping, as he said, the coat's and the petticoat's account distinct, so he proceeded up the common to the usual halting-place; viz., the guide-post, where the Low Thornton and Hemmington roads intersected the waste.

Here was a fresh gathering – the cream of the hunt – the gentlemen who came late, in fact, Newton and Snobson, and Hastler, and Spooner, the two Bibbings, with Spencer Jones, and Burgess and Scarratt, with the usual concomitant grooms. Great were the nudgings, and starings, and what next-ings as the cavalcade approached. The like had never been seen in the Heavyside Hunt.

'Well done, Romford!' exclaimed one.

'Who'd ha' thought it?' muttered another. 'A lady whipper-in,' observed a third.

'A deuced pretty one, too,' observed young Spooner, drawing his horse round to have a good stare at her.

And very pretty she was. Nicely hatted, nicely habited, nicely horsed, nicely arranged altogether.

So thought they all as she passed along, looking down demurely, as if she thought of nobody, and thought nobody thought of her. That of course was a little acting.

'Mornin',' said Facey, 'mornin', mornin',' continued he, giving two or three random shots of nods at the different groups of sportsmen as he passed, several of whom took off their hats to the lady. He then made for a piece of rising ground a little to the left of the guide-post, in order to give his hounds a roll on the greensward prior to throwing off. And as he showed no symptoms of a desire to introduce his fair friend to this the first-class portion of his field either, they renewed their criticisms as soon as the cavalcade was past.

'Why, that's Mrs. Rounding's horse,' observed Jones.

'So it is,' said Mr. Newton. 'Thought there couldn't be two of that colour.'

'They say he's vicious,' observed Hastler.

'Nothing of the sort,' replied Newton. 'Mrs. Rounding has no hand. See! that lady can do what she likes with him,' added he, watching Lucy's light hand, as she twisted and turned the horse about at her will.

'Who is she?' asked Mr. George Bibbing, pressing up.

'Don't know,' answered Hastler, with a shake of the head.

'I do,' observed Jones, with a knowing wink. 'Well, who?' asked several.

The Quorn.
Towards Ashby de la Zouch.
Breedon Church in distance.

'The lady at the "West-end Swell," to be sure,' replied he, after a pause.

'Oh, nonsense,' rejoined Bibbing 'not a bit like her.'

'As like as ladies generally are in hats and habits to what they are in dresses.'

'Well, they do make a great difference to be sure,' observed Snobson, who had mistaken Mrs. for Miss Noakes, once.

'But what is she doing here?' demanded Spooner.

'Better ask the master that,' replied Bibbing.

Facey, however, didn't look at all like a man to take liberties with, as he sat in the midst of his hounds, his little watchful ferrety eyes peeping and peering about in all directions, to 'see how,' as he said, 'the cat jumped.'

Lucy, on her part, took things very quietly, apparently paying more attention to the hounds than watching who was looking at her, though of course she still kept an eye out for admiration. Leotard also behaved most amiably, answering the touch of her light hand on the plain snaffle-bit, now turning Pillager, now following Rummager, as though he were personally interested in the order and decorum of the pack. At length, time being up, – a quarter to eleven, – Facey gave Lucy a nod, and after a widespreading run through the common, a slight twang of the horn brought the hounds to his horse's heels, and away they all jogged for Falcondale Wood.

'You take the high side,' said Facey to Lucy, as they now approached the cover – a long straggling wood, placed on a steepish hill-side. 'You take the high side, and blow this whistle if he breaks,' continued he, giving her a shrill dog-whistle as he spoke; whereupon Lucy scuttled away up the rough side at the east end of the wood, closely followed by sundry swells, who preferred watching her to keeping along the low fields as usual.

'Cover, hoick!' cried Facey to his hounds, with a slight wave of his arm, and in an instant they were tumbling and scrambling head over heels through the blind fence into the wood. Facey, mounted on Brilliant, then rode quietly along on the line, keeping a watchful eye as well on the now wide-spreading pack in the cover as on the Lucy-pressing youths up above. He had only sixteen couple of hounds out, having brought nothing but what he could depend upon.

They had not been in cover many minutes, ere old black-and-tan Vanquisher, who had hurried along a path with a palpable but still unproclaimable scent, struck up a little fern-covered ravine, and as nearly as possible had old Reynard by the neck. But the fox bounced with a desperate energy that aroused the whole pack; a crash sounded through the wood as they hurried together, while the shrill sound of the whistle presently proclaimed he was gone.

Facey got his horse by the head, and cramming into the ragged fence, cleared the wide water-channel beyond, and forced his way up the wooded bank, regardless alike of stubs, briars, and thorns. Another effort over a broad rail-topped mound, with a yawner on the far side, landed him handsomely on farmer Bushell's fallow, just as the hounds, closely followed by Lucy, were straining over the large grass-field beyond. There was a rare scent. Every hound threw his tongue, making the welkin ring with the melody. So they raced up Amerton Hill, past Nutwell grove and Kellerton Law, through Oakley Wood beyond. The pace presently slackened; hunting became more the order of the day, to the satisfaction of the majority of the

'The Wilton on Gallows Hill' by Lionel Edwards. This watercolour and gouache on grey paper shows Edwards' versatility in capturing all aspects of the chase. The mounted field watches as hounds draw for their fox. [By permission of Kenneth Edwards.]

field, who preferred seeing the intricacies of the chase unravelled, to being borne furiously along at a pace that did not allow them to look after anything but themselves.

Thus they hunted steadily past Brackenhill Green, skirting Orton Moor, leaving the Scar on the left, down the banks by the Winwick road, into the Vale of Heatherfield below. Lucy and Facey, or rather Facey and Lucy, kept their places gallantly, Leotard going with the greatest temper and moderation, as though he were the best-behaved horse in the world.

Whatever Facey took, Lucy took; and whatever Lucy took, the young H.H.'s felt constrained to take, for the honour and credit of the hunt. So there was more dashing riding and heavy fencing on this occasion than usual. Romford, to do him justice, was always with his hounds, though Daniel Swig and Chowey both knew how to shirk.

The steady hounds still kept pressing on, carrying the scent over the sandy soil of Heatherfield Vale with laudable pertinacity. This enabled the 'heavy fathers' of the stage – the paterfamilias of the hunt – to come up, and presently the Westham and Studland road resounded with the ringing hoofs of the horses, and the laughing hilarity of the riders, each overjoyed at getting such a near view. And the slower the pace, the more they enjoyed it.

Splendid hounds! Finest run that ever was seen! By Jove! they're away again!' And scarcely had the fatties given their horses the wind, and the youngsters looked down for lost shoes, ere Harmony and Desperate, having got upon a warm headland, gave such a proclamation of satisfaction as brought all their fellows to the enjoyment, making young and old again drop on their reins.

The hunt was up! Facey's round shoulders were again careering in the distance, and Lucy's plump figure was equally conspicuous. So they raced away, the hounds passing handsomely through the deer in Beechborough Park, round Sorrel Hill, past the limekilns at Dewlish, and into Langley Lordship beyond.

And here the first check occurred. The fox had been chased by a shepherd's dog, and the mischief was increased by a complication of sheep. The stupid muttons were just wheeling into line as Facey slipped through the farmyard on the hill.

'Hold hard!' cried he, raising his hand high in the air, to enforce quiet from those behind, while his hounds made their own cast ere he interfered with them. They spread and cast well to the front, to the right, to the left, – but no scent. The fox has been forced back on his line, and the field are all over the ground. The steam of the horses, the chatter of the followers, and the clatter of the roadsters, increase the disaster. Facey sits transfixed, one keen eye watching the hounds, the other raking the country round. At length he sees the black author of the mischief skulking along a hedgerow to his smock-frocked master, who appears at a railing at the far corner of the field.

'Case for a cast,' says Facey to himself; and getting his horse by the head, he halloas 'Turn them,' to Lucy, who forthwith gets round them in a quiet but most masterly manner, and a single twang of Facey's horn, with a crack of her whip, sent them all flying the way Facey wanted them. He then gave them plenty of swing, letting them use their own sagacity as much as possible, and was rewarded at the end of a semicircular cast by hitting off the scent at a meuse.

'The Belvoir', by John King. Author Michael Clayton, left, and artist John King following the Belvoir across the Long Clawson road, heading towards the Belvoir Vale.

'Well done!' 'Devilish well done!' 'Capitally done!' cried the field, more to Lucy than Facey, as the hounds dashed over the fence into the turnip-field beyond, and took up the running inside the hedgerow. Being on turf, with a pleasant vista of white gates before them, the field kept on that tack, and Facey went scuttling along, throwing wide the portals as he passed. The best of friends, however, must part, and the line of gates at length came to an abrupt termination in a very rough, tangled boundary fence between Mr. Pilkington's and Emmerson Gunliffe's farms, at Shepherdswell Hill. It seemed as if it was made up of all the rubbish and refuse of the country, and zig-zagged like a lady's vandyked petticoat, wasting and spoiling a great width of land.

For the first time in the run, Facey changed his mind as he approached the fence, turning from a tangled black thorn lapped with mountain ash, to a still more impervious-looking ivy-blind place.

'Dash it! but this is a rum customer,' said Facey to Lucy, as he stood erect in his stirrups, looking what was on the far side.

'Oh, throw your heart over it,' said Lucy, 'and then follow it as quickly as you can.'

'Heart!' muttered Facey.' I shall never find it again if I do. It would be like lookin' for a needle in a bundle of hay.'

'Let me try, then,' said Lucy, backing Leotard to give him a good run at it. She then put his head straight, gave him a slight touch of the whip and a feel of the spur, and was presently floundering in the thick of the fence.

'I thought how it would be,' said Facey, jumping off his horse, and running to her assistance. But before he got up, another vigorous effort of the horse extricated her from her difficulties, and landed her in the next field, with a considerable quantity of burrs and briars in her habit.

'Well done the lady!' cried the panting Mr. Goldthrop, now coming up, not only pleased, but grateful for the performance.

If Facey would but charge it too, the field might all be able to get through. What a place it was!

And Facey, having clambered back into his saddle, turned his horse quick round, and thrusting his hat down on his brow, claimed his right of saltation. They were all ready to yield him the *pas*, services of danger being generally at a discount, and Romford was presently planted in the midst of the thicket, which Leotard had done little to enlarge. Scramble they went, the horse fighting and struggling as if in the sea, Facey sitting with his feet out of the stirrups, ready to throw himself off clear if required.

It, however, was not necessary, for Brilliant, after many flounders, with a tremendous heave, extricated himself from a woodbine-laced binder that held him, and landed on his nose on the opposite side. He was up like lightning, and Facey, who held on by the mane and his spurs, being chucked back into his seat, gathered himself together, and ere he sat, gave a cheering exclamation of 'There's nothing on the far side!' But if there was nothing on the far side, there was a great deal on theirs, as many of them seem to be aware.

However, it was no time for measuring, and Leotard's friend, Tom Heslop, coming up on a three-parts-broken cart colt, dashed manfully in, and fought a road safely through in the

'Handing it Out to 'Em' c. 1924 by 'Snaffles' (Charlie Johnson Payne), an inimitable study of a young lady jumping a stiff set of and rails in front of the field, with a remarque of a young lady clearing a stone wall. [Courtesy of Felix Rosenstiel's Widow and Son Ltd., London]

HANDING IT OUT TO 'EM.

To Herself
with my best Thanks

miraculous way peculiar to drunken men. What before was all doubt and obscurity, suddenly became clear and transparent. It was then who should get at it first. No 'I'll hold your horse if you'll catch mine,' or friendly negotiation of that sort.

Meanwhile, the hounds had shot sadly away, leaving not a trace of their melody behind; and but for the clubbing of sheep and the staring of cattle, the H. H. gentlemen would hardly have known which way to ride. To be sure, an occasional countryman, after a prolonged stare, in reply to the inquiry if he had seen the hounds, would drawl out, 'Ye-a-s, ar see'd them,' but none of them could muster intelligence enough to answer 'where,' ere the questioner was out of ear-shot. However, they rode on, hopefully and manfully: the young ones, as usual, abusing the fox for taking such a line, the old ones wishing they might come up with them again before they killed.

Fortune, however, always favours the brave, and after clattering through the little straggling straw-thatched village of Reepham, bringing all the women and children to the doors in bewildered astonishment, Mr. Friar's quick eye caught sight of a red-coat topping the edge on the opposite hill, up whose sandy side ran the road they were then pursuing.

'Yonder they go.' cried he, pointing it out with his whip, though he did not know how far the hounds might be ahead of the coat. But riding to anything was better than riding to nothing, galloping about the country, exclaiming, 'Have you seen the hounds?'

They then clattered down Cockenhatch Hill, across the bridge over the rushing stream, and laying hold of their horses' manes, proceeded to stand in their stirrups, and hug them up the opposite bank. That gained, some of the young ones, disdaining the road, dashed over a quickset fence into a heavy fallow, and sought the line Mr. Romford was leading, or rather following, for Lucy was leading. The old ones pounded away on the road, reaching the crown of Eccleston Hill long before the seceders, when their admiring optics were greeted with a sight of the hounds swinging down the green slope of Rippendale Hill, closely followed by Lucy and Facey. Then there was a burst of enthusiasm at the magnificent way the hounds were doing their work, slightly clouded, perhaps, by the sight of the silvery Ribble, meandering its tortuous course through the rich green fields of the vale. What if he should cross it, thought they. However, it was no time for reflection. Meanwhile, Facey and Lucy had got together, and Facey's keen eye descried the fox taking the water, and floating down the stream so as to land a good way below the taking-off place.

'Cunnin' beggar,' said Facey, pointing him out to Lucy; 'but I'll have you in hand for all that,' muttered he.

R.S. Surtees, *Mr Facey Romford's Hounds* (1865)

A LONG RUN

❖

'I tallyhoed the fox away,' said he, 'so of course got a good start. I was on a very quick one, nothing like the best in my stable; in short, *only a five year old*, and not so wise as he should be; but I had had a taste of him, and I could neither blow him nor *funk* him, for he would face any thing. When he was in training – which by the bye was only last year – he was a little queer in his temper, and he never appeared comfortable in a crowd, so that I always, when I could, took a line of my own with him.

'Our first fence this day was a flight of rails, with a yawning ditch on the further side, which I thought it was my luck to have the first fly at; but, looking earnestly at the hounds, as every man should do, you know, I never saw young M—, who came right across me at the fence, and got a nasty sort of a fall (he told me afterwards, he could not hold his mare; if so, all well; if not, *it served him right*).

'I tried to stop the young thorough-bred one; but he threw up his head, and it was "no go"; so, thinking my own the more valuable life of the two – I mean more valuable than young M—'s, – I let him go, and all I saw of young M—, was his mare's belly and his own head, the rest of his body being under the mare. However, I never touched him, I am happy to say, and two others did as I did; but the third was not *quite* so fortunate.

'He jumped on his head, as he thought, but it was only his hat, as his head had just then slipped out of it. But you know, my dear fellow, these things will happen in our fast country.

'No joke, you are aware, for a fellow to fall at the first fence, with such a crowd close behind him, all trying to get first, in fact, all jealous as girls. However, I kept my line; and if I remember right, the next fence was nothing – *only* a gate, a stiff one to be sure; but young ones are always good at timber, that is to say, if they will but look at it; but the pace was beginning to tell already, for the country was most infernally deep.

'There were not more than eight or ten *very* near the hounds, and no one exactly on my line, so I didn't care a rush for a fall. I saw things were going well, and puggy was facing a rare country. In short, we could plainly see we were in for a tickler.

'I began to be sorry, however, that I was riding the young one – indeed I meant to have had him second horse, and I will say this, Wilson advised me to it. However, I let him go; and as I only gave three hundred for him at Newmarket, I thought I'd try what he was made of. You know, my good fellow, it's no use keeping horses to look at at Melton, and if they are good for nothing, send them to the hammer! Let them try their luck in the rurals. You know they won't do for us.

'The next fence was a bullfinch – black as night itself. You could not have seen through it with a lantern. As to what was t'other side Heaven only knew. I could not guess; but what was to be done? The hounds were going the top of the pace, no time to turn a yard right or left;

two fellows rather nearer to them than I was (couldn't bear that you know) so *at it* we went. As for the young one, he absolutely appeared to like it, but I cannot say I did, though I should have thought little of it with most of my other horses, and you know I have near a score about as good as my neighbours. It was a rasper to be sure, and I can't say but I was glad when we were over it.

'The next man to me would not have it at all, but there were five more well with the hounds to my left – all the rest *nowhere*. To be sure the pace was nothing less than terrific. John White sang out – "sharper than common this morning my boy, how does the young one like it?" and you know he seldom cries out on that score.

'Indeed he reminds me of Jem Robinson the jockey. Jem swears a race horse never yet went fast enough for *him*, and declares if it would not hurt him, he should like to be shot out of a cannon's mouth; and so it is with John White and a few others. The pace is scarcely ever good enough for them. However, there was no cause for complaint now.

'My horse kept going well, in short he delighted me. I would not have taken a thousand for him. He jumped an ox-fence – the next but one after the bullfinch – and then a stile with an awkward footbridge, and a brook, quite as well as old Bounce would have jumped them. I have got a trump, quoth I, to *myself*, for there was no one very near to have heard me. The blood of old Prunella will tell. But he kept shaking his head in a curious manner. I had never seen him do so before.

'If I had had my whip in my hand, I should have given him a nobber, for you know it's awkward, going very fast at high and strong timber – post and rail, or what not – with a blind ditch on your side (and you know the ditches in Leicestershire are like all other ditches in November) with your horse shaking his head like a terrier shaking a rat.

'But I had lost my whip at that infernal bullfinch, and part of my breeches too. I know not how it happened, but that day I was not in leathers. I suppose Johnson thinks corderoys less trouble, and often says when he wakes me – "Likely to be wet, sir, better not wear leathers to-day." The sly rogue! the washerwoman polishes the corderoys, but *he* cleans the leathers, you know. However, to proceed with my story. When we checked for a minute or two under Carlton Clump, I found what it was that made the poor devil shake his head. He had got a great thorn in his eye, out of that infernal bullfinch, and the blood was running down the side of his head from a tear from another.

'I got the thorn out the best way I could, but he was evidently in great pain. What was to be done? I could have cried. You know I love horses better than most things, and I abhor cruelty in any shape. I would not it should have happened for a thousand guineas or more.

'But it was done. I looked out for the second horses, not one was to be seen; and how should they? We had come as straight as a bird could have flown, for at least six miles. I condemned myself; I wished myself any where but where I was, I said – "What could have possessed me to have ridden Edwin first horse to-day, in such a country as this, when Footpad is so fit to go, and Wilson told me I'd better not.

"I'll go home," I said; but confound it, – at that very moment Ravisher and Rantipole hit off the scent, and, my good fellow, what could I do? What would you have done? Edwin had

'The Finest View in Europe', 1921, by 'Snaffles' is probably his most famous sporting print. There were many different versions over a ten year period of this view of a fence and hounds beyond, from the back of a grey horse. The remarque here shows a fence-layer raising his hand as a holloa. [Courtesy of Felix Rosenstiel's Widow and Son Ltd., London]

recovered his wind, and as he shook his head less, and played cheerfully with his bit, I hoped he was better.

He was carrying me *magnificently*; not more than a dozen fellows with the hounds; a splendid country before us – *I took the lead again*; I shall never forget the third fence we now came to, which was out of the next field but one to Shankton Holt. It was not a *double*, but a *treble* (a *trouble* I was going to say). It was of this description, but thank heaven there are not many such. There was first a ditch, then a rail, then another ditch, and then another rail. You see there is no landing for a horse if he takes this at twice, except on the first rail, or in the second ditch; but the old ones *will* double these fences when very well handled too.

'But the wind was in Edwin and I knew he would face anything, but I doubted his being up to this queer double. I sent him at it, then, at the rate of forty miles an hour, thinking to clear it all; but, far as the clever young horse could fling himself, he could not clear the whole. He alighted with one fore leg over, and the other under the outermost rail, and gave me a thundering fall. "It's unfortunate," said I to myself, glancing my eye at the fence, as I arose from the ground, "if I had known that middle rail had been so weak, we should have gone in

THE FINEST VIEW IN EUROPE

and out clever – at least with only a scramble. I'm out of luck today," added I, "but here goes again," and soon jumped into my saddle.

'The hounds turning to me a little, I was almost immediately in my place again. "What now?" said one. "Disasters come thickly this morning," cried another. "All right again," replied I; take care of yourselves, for we are in for business to-day, and I perceive one or two of you have been kissing your Mother Earth.

'Don't holloaa till you're out of the wood, my boys! The scent appeared better and better; indeed, the pace had been awful since the check in the windmill-field. I looked back twice, and could only see four, and there were but five besides myself with the hounds. "This is beautiful," I said. "*Divine!*" shouted L. I thought so too. I could not help giving them a cheer which I don't often do.'

Charles James Apperley ('Nimrod'), *Nimrod's Hunting Reminiscences* (1843)

'Pride cometh' 1912, is the first part of a self-portrait by 'Snaffles' looking spruce in part one at the opening meet of the Cottesmore on his ex-hurdler The Colonel which he nicknamed Flash Harry. See page 147 for part two. [Courtesy of Felix Rosenstiel's Widow and Son Ltd., London]

PHILIPPA'S FOX HUNT

❖

There, suddenly, were the hounds, scrambling in baffled silence down into the road from the opposite bank, to look for the line they had overrun, and there, amazingly, was Philippa, engaged in excited converse with several men with spades over their shoulders.

'Did ye see the fox, boys?' shouted Flurry, addressing the group.

'We did! we did!' cried my wife and her friends in chorus; 'he ran up the road!'

'We'd be badly off without Mrs. Yeates!' said Flurry, as he whirled his mare round and clattered up the road with a hustle of hounds after him.

It occurred to me as forcibly as any mere earthly thing can occur to those who are wrapped in the sublimities of a run, that, for a young woman who had never before seen a fox out of a cage at the Zoo, Philippa was taking to hunting very kindly. Her cheeks were a most brilliant pink, her blue eyes shone.

'Oh, Sinclair!' she exclaimed, 'they say he's going for Aussolas, and there's a road I can ride all the way!'

'Ye can, Miss! Sure we'll show you!' chorused her *cortège*.

Her foot was on the pedal ready to mount. Decidedly my wife was in no need of assistance from me.

Up the road a hound gave a yelp of discovery, and flung himself over a stile into the fields; the rest of the pack went squealing and jostling after him, and I followed Flurry over one of those infinitely varied erections, pleasantly termed 'gaps' in Ireland. On this occasion the gap was made of three razor-edged slabs of slate leaning against an iron bar, and Sorcerer conveyed to me his thorough knowledge of the matter by a lift of his hind-quarters that made me feel as if I were being skilfully kicked downstairs. To what extent I looked it, I cannot say, nor providentially can Philippa, as she had already started. I only know that undeserved good luck restored to me my stirrup before Sorcerer got away with me in the next field.

What followed was, I am told, a very fast fifteen minutes; for me time was not; the empty fields rushed past uncounted, fences came and went in a flash, while the wind sang in my ears, and the dazzle of the early sun was in my eyes. I saw the hounds occasionally, sometimes pouring over a green bank, as the charging breaker lifts and flings itself, sometimes driving across a field, as the white tongues of foam slide racing over the sand; and always ahead of me was Flurry Knox, going as a man goes who knows his country, who knows his horse, and whose heart is wholly and absolutely in the right place.

Do what I would, Sorcerer's implacable stride carried me closer and closer to the brown mare, till, as I thundered down the slope of a long field, I was not twenty yards behind Flurry.

Sorcerer had stiffened his neck to iron, and to slow him down was beyond me; but I fought his head away to the right, and found myself coming hard and steady at a stonefaced bank with broken ground in front of it.

Flurry bore away to the left, shouting something that I did not understand. That Sorcerer shortened his stride at the right moment was entirely due to his own judgment; standing well away from the jump, he rose like a stag out of the tussocky ground, and as he swung my twelve stone six into the air the obstacle revealed itself to him and me as consisting not of one bank but of two, and between the two lay a deep grassy lane, half choked with furze.

I have often been asked to state the width of the bohereen, and can only reply that in my opinion it was at least eighteen feet; Flurry Knox and Dr. Hickey, who did not jump it, say that it is not more than five.

What Sorcerer did with it I cannot say; the sensation was of a towering flight with a kick back in it, a biggish drop, and a landing on cee-springs, still on the downhill grade. That was how one of the best horses in Ireland took one of Ireland's most ignorant riders over a very nasty place.

A sombre line of fir-wood lay ahead, rimmed with a grey wall, and in another couple of minutes we had pulled up on the Aussolas road, and were watching the hounds struggling over the wall into Aussolas demesne.

'No hurry now,' said Flurry, turning in his saddle to watch the Cockatoo jump into the road, 'he's to ground in the big earth inside. Well, Major, it's well for you that's a big-jumped horse. I thought you were a dead man a while ago when you faced him at the bohereen!'

I was disclaiming intention in the matter when Lady Knox and the others joined us.

'I thought you told me your wife was no sportswoman,' she said to me, critically scanning Sorcerer's legs for cuts the while, 'but when I saw her a minute ago she had abandoned her bicycle and was running across country like—'

' Look at her now!' interrupted Miss Sally. 'Oh! – oh!' In the interval between these exclamations my incredulous eyes beheld my wife in mid-air, hand in hand with a couple of stalwart country boys, with whom she was leaping in unison from the top of a bank on to the road.

Every one, even the saturnine Dr. Hickey, began to laugh; I rode back to Philippa, who was exchanging compliments and congratulations with her escort.

'Oh, Sinclair!' she cried, 'wasn't it splendid? I saw you jumping, and everything! Where are they going now?'

'My dear girl,' I said, with marital disapproval, 'you're killing yourself. Where's your bicycle?'

'Oh, its punctured in a sort of lane, back there. It's all right; and then they' – she breathlessly waved her hand at her attendants – 'they showed me the way.'

'Begor! you proved very good, Miss!' said a grinning cavalier.

'Faith she did!' said another, polishing his shining brow with his white flannel coat-sleeve, 'she lepped like a haarse!'

'And may I ask how you propose to go home?' said I.

'I don't know and I don't care! I'm not going home!' She cast an entirely disobedient eye at me. 'And your eye-glass is hanging down your back and your tie is bulging out over your waistcoat!'

The little group of riders had begun to move away.

'We're going on into Aussolas,' called out Flurry; 'come on, and make my grandmother give you some breakfast, Mrs. Yeates; she always has it at eight o'clock.'

E. OE. Somerville and Martin Ross, *Some Experiences of an Irish R. M.* (1899)

MY TOP-HAT TRICK.

CHARLIE

— ❖ —

So there is life after politics, and, in my case, unsurprisingly, this has quite a lot to do with horses. To my eye a mature and well conformed thoroughbred horse is the most beautiful creature on earth. To behold a stallion like Royal Academy for instance is to catch your breath. His presence provides an intellectual satisfaction, a feeling of exhilaration which lasts well after the horse has returned to his box. To watch them grow from foals to yearlings in our paddocks gives a pleasure which mercifully compensates for the all too possible disappointment and sense of loss when, sadly, they leave us for the sale ring.

Keats has it that beauty equals truth and vice versa, indeed he says that is all we need to know about life. It is an attractive idea but alas does not apply to horses, or the bookmakers would long ago have left the business. Yet just sometimes it holds good.

It was on a Friday in January, 1980, near Lowesby in Leicestershire that I first met Charlie. I was in urgent need of a good quality hunter and the need had been placed in the ever capable hands of my friend George Rich, a brilliant horseman and a dealer who had a genius for fitting horses to people. He was riding a tough looking chestnut with a lovely head.

'I think you'd better sit on this one' he said. I looked again. The horse seemed small for me and I said so. 'I think he's got a bit of a motor,' said George. 'Hurry up, you can have 'im for twenty minutes, there's another after him.' George generally said that. We swapped over. I found I had a minor earthquake beneath me.

'What's his name?' I asked.

'We call him Charlie.'

With that I heard the horn, hounds were away and there was no more time to enquire into Charlie's antecedents. Indeed no time for anything except to try to steer him.

Lowesby is a lovely bit of rolling grass country scored with stout hedges and rails. We were heading for a stout hedge. Charlie had taken a decision about this without reference to me. We whizzed over it, shot past several surprised and hard-riding horsemen and found ourselves lined up for a fairly solid set of rails. My attempt to check Charlie was unavailing. I left him to it.

He met the fence on the wrong stride and decided to ignore it, he simply galloped through it. Splintered pieces of rail shot into the air. I tensed for the inevitable somersault. Charlie barely checked his stride, on we went. At the end of twenty minutes I had lost George and nearly caused several accidents, not least to myself.

Somewhere near White's Barn there was a merciful check. Charlie, clearly irritated at this unnecessary interruption, turned round in circles, throwing up his handsome, intelligent head, ears pricked, lower lip trembling with perpetual excitement.

George appeared. 'Do you want him?' he asked. I was in two very different minds. On the

'The Berkeley near Rockhampton', watercolour by Lionel Edwards – a superbly executed impression of the Berkeley field tackling the formidable open water ditches, known as rheens, in its deep-riding vale country by the Severn. [By permission of Kenneth Edwards.]

one hand here was a horse full of matchless courage and enthusiasm, on the other, I had only one neck.

'He doesn't know much,' I said.

'He'll learn,' said George. 'He's got a motor.'

It turned out Charlie was just five years old, had inevitably come over from Ireland, and then been sold, 'to a man in the north who couldn't get on with him'. I had some sympathy with the 'man in the north'. Charlie was by an Irish thoroughbred stallion called Prince Rhoy. No one knew who his mother was, or if they did they weren't telling. 'He jumped that big drop fence superb,' said George. I guessed that George had fitted him to me. Filled with many versions of reasonable doubt, I said, 'O.K.'

Sir Stephen Hastings, *Drums of Memory* (1994)

HUNTERS

❖

To enjoy hunting it is absolutely essential to be well mounted. A friend of mine married for a horse; a very sensible thing to do. Her most ardent suitor had mounted her on his superlative hunter for one whole season, at the end of which he suggested that it was time that she made up her mind whether she would marry him or not. She realised that if she said 'no' she could hardly expect him to produce her favourite animal for her any more; so it had to be 'yes'. Unfortunately, the horse broke down and never hunted again – but the marriage was a great success. Well I suppose it is as good a reason for getting married as any other.

I advocated in *Horse & Hound* buying horses from reputable dealers, rather than from friends, as this is apt to end beautiful friendships. The next week I met Simon Clarke, then Master of the Cottesmore, from whom I had bought a hunt horse that autumn. Simon said to me quite huffily, 'I thought that horse was a success – or did you never consider we were friends?'

I have always liked big horses, especially with the rough people there are around today. In fact I consider a big good one is better than a good little one.

The best horse I ever rode was Cottage Point who originally belonged to James Hanbury. Sold at auction he had a short and very unsuccessful sojourn in the Heythrop country. (Possibly like me he fancied Leicestershire!) John Smith-Maxwell, who was living at Moreton-in-the Marsh, rang us up to tell us that the new owners wanted to get rid of Cottage Point at any price; so Tony bought him, (through John) for less than half what he had fetched at auction.

The first time I rode Cottage, I was waiting while someone jumped a post and rails, when to my surprise Cottage leaped about ten foot in the air, took two strides in the other direction and jumped a place I should never have considered negotiable. This is quite a horse, I thought, and quickly annexed him as mine.

He was the bravest horse I ever rode, with the biggest jump, he never put in a short stride, just stood off any distance. He never looked where he was landing (which was sometimes a pity!) but on to where he could jump the next fence. He had an absolute passion for jumping, and if he saw anyone else jump an obstacle he just took off, giving the most enormous leap in sympathy. This entailed keeping a sharp look out which way he was pointing or some unsuspecting chum would be either knocked off his horse or knocked over, which was not always tremendously popular. Cottage would not ever wait his turn, but luckily for me, when I said, 'WHOA Cottage', everyone seemed to get out of the way.

As a matter of fact it can be very advantageous to ride a horse that won't wait, but it is absolutely maddening if other people do!

Cottesmore huntsman Neil Coleman showing how to jump a daunting over-grown cut and laid fence with a ditch before. Going first over obstacles however large is part of a huntsman's skills too often taken for granted by mounted followers who usually have a lead over fences. (Photo: Jim Meads, My Hunting World)

Before the foreigners spoiled the market, I used to get horses from Ireland. Boodley Daresbury was a wonderful judge of a horse, and had many contacts round Limerick. She used to find good quality hunters which made a habit of flying the banks, and were therefore rather a dangerous ride in Ireland. She would buy them and ring up one of her many friends in England who would be quite prepared to buy a horse 'blind' if Boodley recommended it.

It was always tremendous fun staying at Clonshire with the Daresburys and going horse coping with Boodley, though I must admit I was not madly keen on being forced to ride her own young horses, prior to our expedition, and even before breakfast. I remember one morning having just returned from the most hazardous ride, Boodley said, 'Now we must ride the green ones.' In horror I asked, 'What on earth do you call the ones we have just ridden?' 'Oh, they have been backed a month', she explained, 'the next lot have only been ridden for ten days.'

On one occasion we met a stationary ass cart in a grass lane. It required all our combined powers of persuasion and intrepid horsemanship to induce our mounts to sidle past. When this was finally accomplished Boodley turned to me and said proudly, 'You see they are all right with traffic.'

In County Cork a charming man took us round to look at some likely animals. Boodley, I found, had told him that I was so poor that unless he could produce a very cheap, but naturally brilliant horse, I would not be able to afford to hunt at all. It was a sad story and brought tears to his eyes; but when we bid him goodbye, he told me how pleased he was to have met me as he had seen so many pictures of me and my husband in *Horse & Hound*. (Tony was Master of the Quorn at the time). I was very embarrassed, feeling that if by chance he had believed it all, he must have thought Tony extremely mean! Boodley was unrepentant, and thought it a perfectly natural thing to have said.

Some years later Migs Greenall and I were staying at Clonshire, and Boodley took us out for a really hilarious day buying horses. One of the first animals we saw was quite a nice grey, which we wished to try, but unfortunately although we had brought a saddle with us, no bridle could be found. Finally, we discovered a cart horse bridle, complete with blinkers, which was broken at the top and tied together with pink ribbon. But it had no reins and Boodley was quite cross when neither Migs nor I would consent to ride without any, despite the fact that Boodley offered to lead the grey with her hand on the bit. In the end some binder twine was produced in place of reins, so all was well. Boodley bought the horse and named him Binder Twine.

The next animal we saw was small and black; his owner insisted on trotting him very fast over cobble stones in the yard, and jumping him over a single strand of wire back and forth. There was nowhere else to try him, and it did not strike me as typical of the Quorn country, but I bought him. He was called Brandy; I added 'Soda' and after hunting and then jumping him for one year, I sold him at a nice profit as a jumper. George Hobbs jumped him internationally with great success.

We saw many horses that day, finishing up in the dark at some deserted stables, where a note

Phil Arthers, Joint Master of the Meynell and South Staffs, one of the most admired field masters in the Midlands, gives a firm lead over a hedge. (Photo: Jim Meads, My Hunting World)

had been left for us, thoughtfully placed with a torch, saying, 'The mare you want to see is in the second box on the left'.

We got her out and I trotted her up in the pitch dark yard, while Boodley and Migs looked at her in the wavering beam of light from the torch. Migs, I thought rather bravely, bought her on the telephone later that night, without any idea what she looked like. However she was sent over to Migs in England and turned out to be a success.

Latterly I have bought horses in England. Robin Leyland provided me with some very good ones; he was always very expansive about their faults. 'He is sure to buck you off,' he would say, or, 'You will never hold him, but he might do Michael', or, 'You won't like the look of her, but she does jump.'

Great Expectations, who I bought from Eric Wright, was very nappy, and nobody liked her except me, but I adored her; she was brilliant. Since she broke down she has bred two very nice foals for Frank Hewitt, who has her now.

Hobson's Choice came from George Rich, and I have in fact, ridden him on 270 days hunting during the last six seasons. He is a great character; never misses a day, never puts a foot wrong, and adores hunting.

Aquarius who was given to me by Peter Pritchard, (one of the nicest and most unexpected presents I have ever had) was the ideal stamp of hunter to my mind, size, scope, quality as well as ability. Later I bought The Harbourer which Michael rides, from Peter Pritchard and he is a super bright chestnut horse.

John Betteridge sold me a beautiful big horse which I think is a bit extra. But just when I had solved a slight brakes problem, and was delighted with him, we had a very nasty accident when his hind legs fell through a concealed and very deep drain at Prestwold. I have not been able to ride him since, so I hope when he has recovered next year, he will prove as brilliant as I think.

But I could go on about my horses forever!

Ulrica Murray Smith MFH, Magic of the Quorn (1980)

THE FUN OF IT

—— ❖ ——

We are in for a marvellous tour today. Hounds scream away above the village of Braunston, swing left, and run hard southwards, parallel to the Wisp, the long straight road to Braunston from Withcote. We jump timber rails out of tufty old turf; we steady our horses as best we can, for this is a wet season, with deep going. There are calls from the Field Master to 'keep in'; we must be careful to mark the pastures as little as possible, so we ride close to the hedgerows.

At the rear of the field are two riders in tweed coats; their job is to ensure that farm gates are all closed, but everyone in the field is mindful of this obligation. We have a Hunt fence mender out on the roads in a van; he will repair any rails broken by a jumping horse, or fill in any gaps in hedges.

Half way alongside a tributary of the Gwash, we find the only way ahead is to cross this brook; it is narrow, but the banks are steep, clad in brambles, and decidedly trappy. Rosemary Samworth's horse slides carefully down half-way, and leaps to the opposite steep bank.

We follow one by one, some horses making a neater job than others. My grey mare, Lucy, is marvellous at such obstacles, a skill she learned in her youth in Ireland, and she deals with the brook with reassuring ease. We breast a swell of land to look down on the beautiful Withcote estate, owned by Captain and Mrs Michael Cavenagh.

They are both experienced riders, and their estate is well fitted with jumps for horse trials and hunter trials. Hooray! Hounds are swooping down over the Withcote grass, still speaking; clearly we are hunting a travelling dog fox, making a far point.

We gallop downhill, pull our horses back to take on a timber fence not to be trifled with, and then hurtle down to jump a gate into a field short of the beautiful Withcote manor house.

Still hounds surge ahead, and we gallop across grass to Lover's Walk, the narrow path which runs alongside the narrow River Chater, and past the ruins of Sauvey Castle; an eerie spot this, where it is all too easy to conjure up scenes of bloody battles in pre-history, up to medieval times. This is an ancient settlement, and the old moat and wrecked ramparts are evidence of the need for defence against marauders in England's turbulent past.

No time for reflection now; hounds are running south alongside the stream; we jump a timber fence from all-too slippery mud, ride past the castle's mound, and into the lane from Whatborough crossroads to Launde.

Again our hearts are lifted as hounds run without check across the lane, and over the swell of another Rutland undulation. The field, now somewhat reduced to about forty riders, continues to follow hounds; sometimes leaping timber, sometimes stopping while an electric fence is by-passed, always with as much care as possible for the land we are so fortunate to be able to rider over, thanks to the co-operation of farmers and landowners. This is sheep and cattle country, and we are especially careful to keep well clear of grazing flocks.

We take to the lane to Oxey Farm now as hounds run above us, attended by Neil Coleman and his whipper-in. There is a check; hounds feather over the grass; now they have it again, and run ahead. They swing right, and they are skirting Robin a 'Tiptoe Hill. This owes its name to the felon who was hanged from a tree on top of the hill. They left him overnight swinging from the bough, but it bent and he was able to keep alive by standing on tip toe. Next morning he was found still alive, and was pardoned. Hounds check here. The huntsman casts them widely, but they are unable to pick up the scent. The fox is given best; most of the horses are showing signs of having performed a lot of work in heavy going.

Those of us with second horses, change them at Whatborough crossroads where the horse boxes are gathered. Hounds are taken to draw Owston Woods, the famous covert whose boggy environs have sucked shoes off horses for generations while hounds hunt whole families of foxes up and down the dense woodland. The wood is said to be 'paved with horseshoes and riders' curses'. It is a reminder of the great hunting forests which once dominated the East Midlands when the stag, not the fox, was the premier beast of the Chase.

The major problem for the huntsman is to eject a fox into the open, and to sustain the pressure so that it runs far from the wood instead of skirting back all too quickly. The problem for the mounted field is to be at the right part of the wood's circumference when hounds go away. It is all too easy to miss a run. On this occasion hounds hunt enthusiastically in Owston Big Wood for an hour, while the small mounted field wait patiently at various points around the wood in the hope of holloaing away a fox. We get one brief excursion, but the fox doubles back to the wood after three fields.

Then the huntsman goes to the Preston Lodge side of the Withcote lane which bisects the wood. This is Little Owston, a much more likely place for a run in the open. Hounds chime away with a great cry; we see a fox steal away from the covert to cross the Oakham to Tilton road, but not a hound follows. They are intent on the line of another inside covert. I ride round the covert, and hack slowly round its northern edge. Hounds are speaking on my right. At the far end from the lane there is small knot of riders, David and Rosemary Samworth and two others. They motion me to keep quiet, and we watch a fox running up the hedgerow towards Cheseldyne. Then there is a crash of hound music, and the huntsman sounds the thrilling notes of 'Gone away!' It never fails to make the hairs stand up on the back of my neck.

The Cottesmore hounds surge out of covert on the line of the fox. They run to the left of the next covert, Cheseldyne, and head over the grass towards Ladywood, lying below the fold of hills overlooking Braunston. We jump several sets of rails, and canter across the grass towards Ladywood, the famous covert and the white faced house next to it where Brian and Libby Fanshawe live. Our horses splosh down through the muddy banks of the stream below Ladywood. We canter over the Knossington lane, and wait while hounds scream through the Ladywood covert to our left.

Yes, they are away, and we are in the heaven of grass and fences above Ladywood. My

The Duke of Beaufort's mounted field, wearing their distinctive blue and buff coats, moving off in front of Badminton house at the last Saturday meet before the hunting ban, on February 12, 2005. (Photo: John Minoprio).

chestnut gelding, Hughie, is pulling like a train; he adores hounds, and knows full well that he is in for a good hunt.

Hounds run towards Braunston above the Knossington lane. We jump timber, and some of the delectable fly fences which criss-cross the old turf. The going is very wet, but Hughie makes nothing of it, springing in great arcs over the clipped hedges, and landing far out over the Cottesmore scoops which guard them. If a horse lands in one, or puts his feet into one on take off, it can bring him down, especially when the going is heavy.

Hounds check by the Leicestershire lane; this is a narrow field lane which the mounted field cross by jumping hedges or timber in a somewhat tricky in and out. The huntsman goes back to a knot of hounds feathering in the open; suddenly they are running hard up the hill. We enjoy more grass and fences in pursuit.

Dusk is coming in fast against a band of scarlet and amber sunset. Ahead the shadows are lengthening away from Orton Park Wood covert. The pack runs into the covert, and we scamper round the edge. Hounds are running through the covert on our left. Has the fox gone on towards Cold Overton or Ranksborough?

When hounds emerge from the covert they falter and dwell, casting again on the grass. The fox may have run ahead, but it has gained much valuable time. Darkness is coming fast, and the Master decides it is time to blow for home.

There are now about six riders in the hunt. We say our goodnights and warmest thanks, and I hack back with Andrew and Jane Collie, down over the grass towards Withcote. It is dark when I walk Hughie towards the welcoming glow from the barn door where Mick Smith is giving the horses their evening feed.

The evening hunt lasted only thirty-five minutes; the point was no more than two and half miles, although we covered more than that, but the 'quick thing' remains one of Leicestershire's greatest delights – and to enjoy such a hunt in the late twentieth century in an area which has nurtured foxhunting at its best for over two hundred and fifty years is a remarkable testament to the loyalty which the sport has secured through good times and bad.

Our progress across country, traversing entirely privately owned land, was achieved by a marvellous mixture of old loyalties and friendships, careful liaison, and a country tradition that has miraculously survived all the social upheavals of the twentieth century.

Paradise is not lost.

Michael Clayton, *Foxhunting in Paradise* (1993)